THE RIGHT MATE

THE RIGHT MATE

James Robison
with Jimmie Cox

Tyndale House
Publishers, Inc.
Wheaton, Illinois

Library of Congress
Catalog Card Number
79-55753
ISBN, 0-8423-5599-5 paper.
Copyright © 1979 by James
Robison. All rights reserved.
Third printing, October 1980.
Printed in the United States
of America.

CONTENTS

PART ONE

THE RIGHT DATE

INTRODUCTION

Dating is a part of life. This is the first thing that parents and young people should understand. Dating *is* a part of life. It involves you totally—mentally, physically, and spiritually. It plays an important role in the decision making process that a young person goes through in choosing a lifetime partner. Dating affects every aspect of your life, present and future, and it draws upon every facet of your life.

Since dating is so important a part of life, parents and young people make a serious mistake when they try to isolate dating and look at it as though it were something casual or trivial, and not a phase of life requiring careful thought and preparation. The greatest mistake you can make, Mom and Dad, is to let your daughter or son more or less drift into dating. Many of the broken marriages and shattered families that we see today are the result of just such a careless attitude toward dating. Poor preparation for dating can lead to a lifetime of unfulfilled expectations, unhappiness and misery.

For dating to be a wholesome, beneficial experience, a boy or girl must enter into it well fortified with certain basic truths and wide awake to the danger of disregarding them.

ONE
THE RIGHT OUTLOOK ON LIFE

One of the most important truths a boy or girl must
understand before dating is that a true concept of life is
essential to a wholesome dating experience.

Now I know that sounds pretty heavy, pretty deep, and
philosophical. But the truth is that everyone has a philosophy
whether he realizes it or not. Everyone has some idea
concerning what life's all about.

For Christians, the true concept of life is presented in the
Bible. It can be found stated in many different ways in many
passages of Scripture. One verse that expresses it very
completely and clearly is 1 John 1:3:

"That which we have seen and heard declare we unto you,
that ye also may have fellowship with us: and truly our
fellowship is with the Father, and with his Son Jesus Christ.'

The primary mission of life for the Christian is to spread the
word to others about the Christian experience—something he
or she has "seen and heard." That experience, of course, is the
saving grace of the Lord Jesus Christ.

But the verse also reveals that this mission is not an end in
itself, but only the means to an end. The ultimate purpose of
the Christian life is fellowship. Fellowship with other
Christians. Fellowship with God and the Lord Jesus Christ.
You see, God created man originally for fellowship. He meant
for them, male and female, to have fellowship with one

another. In fact, God revealed his intent concerning fellowship when he made the woman, saying: "It is not good that the man should be alone; I will make him a help meet [a companion] for him" (Genesis 2:18). God derived pleasure and satisfaction from this fellowship with the man and woman, just as they drew fulfillment from their fellowship with him. Genesis 3:8 indicates that a highlight of the day for God and for the man and woman was a leisurely stroll together through the Garden in the cool of the day.

Of course, we all know the story of the tragic breaking of that fellowship by the disobedience of the man and woman. And we know how God made it possible, through the sinless life, death and resurrection of Christ, for that fellowship to be restored, "by grace, through faith" (Eph. 2:8).

But Satan and the tantalizing distractions of the world make it easy for Christians to forget that their real purpose in life is fellowship with God. Satan and the world tell us that the only worthwhile pursuit in life is to get all the pleasure you can. Go out and have all the fun you can. Satisfy all your desires. Life goes around only once, as a TV commercial says, so "grab for all the gusto you can get."

That's the perfect picture of the life that's lived totally for self. It's the portrait of the completely self-centered person. There's no place in the picture for God, much less for fellowship with God. Those who pattern their lives after that picture will spend their years chasing the satisfaction, the fulfillment that the Devil and the world falsely promise them. They'll burn themselves out and destroy themselves in quest of it, and they'll find only bitter disappointment and disillusionment. The promises of the world and of the Devil are lies. The gratification of every basic desire of the physical nature is not the secret to happiness and fullfillment. God bluntly refutes that idea in 1 Corinthians 6:13, where he inspires the Apostle Paul to write: "The body is not for fornication . . ."

That explains many of the problems young people—and, of course, adults—find themselves entangled in today. They are living entirely for self-gratification through the physical stimulation of illicit sex. That's not the purpose of their lives; that's not what the body is meant for.

What is the body meant for? What is the purpose of life? The remainder of the verse quoted above says, ". . . but for the Lord." It reads: "The body is not for fornication, but for the Lord, and the Lord for the body." Fellowship. That's what your body is designed for, and that's the purpose of your life—fellowship with other Christians and fellowship with God.

Now do you see, Mom and Dad, how important it is for your sons and daughters to understand what life is really all about before they go out on a date? Think what the world and the society all around you are telling your young people about what they should have in mind when they start dating. Then ask yourselves, "How does any of this get my child ready for Christian fellowship as an adult, for fellowship with other believers and with God?" Young person, what are your non-Christian friends feeding you concerning what dating is all about? What values do the kids at your school associate with dating? Do their ideas about dating have anything to do with Christian fellowship, with fellowship with Jesus Christ?

Parents, before you give your son or daughter permission to start dating, you have a Christian responsibility to be sure that young person has a clear, unshakable understanding of the true concept of life, as revealed in the Scriptures. Young man, young lady, don't start dating until you understand that your basic reason for living is to have fellowship with other Christians and with God.

Life is for fellowship—with other Christians and with God. Dating is a part of the totality of life. Therefore, dating should be entered into as an activity that forms a part of our fellowship with other Christians and with God, one that cultivates and strengthens that fellowship.

TWO
THE RIGHT TIME

The second truth that needs to be understood is that marriage is for mature people. Dating is part of the maturing process. It helps young people to grow up psychologically, emotionally, and spiritually while they're growing up physically.

You know something about physical maturity, young person. Everyone does. If you're a young man, you know that no sixth-grade athlete has ever made it as a linebacker for the Dallas Cowboys. It's not that no kid that young has ever fantasized and dreamed about wearing that glorious silver and blue uniform. It's not that playing for the Cowboys wouldn't be a great thing to do. It's simply that a sixth-grade boy's body isn't ready to handle the assignment. The sixth-grader who wants to play for the Cowboys just has to face one big, sobering fact: He's got to wait until he grows up physically. Playing for the Cowboys is a man's job. It's not for boys.

The same is true of marriage. Marriage demands physical maturity so that the husband and wife will be capable of performing their basic roles in the relationship—he the role of holding a man's job to support the family, she of bearing and rearing the children and doing the physical tasks involved in maintaining a neat, pleasant home for the family.

The need to grow psychologically and emotionally is not quite as obvious as the need to grow physically, but it's every bit as important. Maturing psychologically means looking on

life from an adult perspective. It means knowing what is most
important in life, what is of little importance, what is least
important and what isn't important at all. To be emotionally
mature means being able and willing to choose to put the
important things first in life, and to do them, when it seems
that things of little or no importance would be more fun to do.
People who don't grow up psychologically and emotionally
are forever getting mixed up about what's important and what
isn't. Or, if they know what's important, they can't bring
themselves to do the important things, because they won't say
"no" to themselves. They insist on doing what they please,
whether it's important or not, whether it's good for them or
bad.

A marriage with one psychologically or emotionally
immature partner is in trouble. A marriage with two immature
partners is doomed. The importance of maturity can't be
overemphasized.

Spiritual maturity is the most important aspect of maturity.
In fact, it forms the foundation for psychological and emtion-
al maturity.

To be spiritually mature, you first have to be spiritually
born. You have to repent of your sins and accept Jesus Christ
and God's forgiveness through him.

The second thing necessary for spiritual maturity is the
surrender of your life to Christ, letting him be Master of your
life, letting him have complete control over it. If that surrender
is real and genuine, you will attend to the other things that
will help you grow spiritually. You will consistently study
your Bible, pray, meditate on God's Word and his will for your
life, tell others about Christ, and diligently learn to serve God
and others.

The third step in spiritual maturity is what the Bible calls
"the peace that passeth understanding." It's the serenity and
stability that comes when you have dared to live by faith and
have found God to be true to his promises.

The mark of immaturity is selfishness. Spiritual growth
tends to destroy self-centeredness and open the door for the rich,
lasting fellowship with others. And that includes the intimate
fellowship of marriage. The destruction of selfishness is the
heart of Christianity. Jesus said, "If any man will come after

me, let him deny himself . . ." That's the first step in the
Christian walk—the denying of self.

Marriages are built on true love—God's kind of love—and
that kind of love can't coexist in the same person with
selfishness. C.W. Brister, a professor of pastoral ministry at one
of the country's leading seminaries, stated this point well in his
book *It's Tough Growing Up*. He said: "True love grows out
of healthy self-regard and generous giving, not uncontrollable
urges." So many young people get the idea from the society
they live in that love is getting: "I want you. I've got to have
you. Give me your love." But the Bible tells us it's just the
other way around. Love is giving. "God so loved . . . that he
gave . . . " (John 3:16). The person who is always getting can't
give. That's why the selfish person can't love—not in the true
sense of the word. And, since the foundation of marriage is
true love, that's why marriages between selfish persons have
little chance of surviving and practically no chance of
producing fulfillment and happiness.

Young person, you must grow spiritually, you must be
spiritually mature before you marry. And it is the parents'
responsibility to see that their children grow and mature
spiritually during the dating period. They should mature
spiritually as they mature physically if their marriage is to be a
stable one producing a home that glorifies God.

One well-known Bible teacher offers this explanation of
spiritual maturity:

When we receive Jesus Christ as our personal Savior, his
Spirit comes to live in our lives. His specific dwelling place is
our human spirit, which he brings to life when he comes in.
(Eph. 1:13, 14)

The Spirit of Christ desires freedom to fill all the inward
parts of the soul—that is, our mind, will, and emotions. He
wants to transform us completely so that the image of Christ
will shine out from our lives. (Eph. 5:18, 19; Rom. 12:2)

When the Holy Spirit reveals thoughts, words, actions or
attitudes that need changing (because they don't conform to
the image of Christ), a test ensues. God's Spirit challenges our
human spirit. If our willful spirit prevails, God's Spirit is
grieved and his effectiveness in us is quenched. (1 Pet. 1:6;
James 1:2; 1 Pet. 4:12; Luke 4:1)

Just as Jesus Christ resisted Satan with the Word of God, the sword of the Spirit, so we must meet each of these tests with truths from God's Word.

To the degree that we cooperate with the Holy Spirit and choose to live by the instructions and promises of God, we develop spiritual maturity.

You can see how important it is to study the Bible and seek God's will through prayer in order to grow up spiritually. It is the Holy Spirit living within us who teaches us and brings to our memory all things that God has said to us. The more we let God say to us, through reading and studying the Bible, the more weapons the Holy Spirit has to choose from in protecting us from temptation and guiding us in the way in which God would have us to walk.

A final word concerning maturity—and it's the one that impatient young people usually hate to hear: Maturing takes time. If you're a young person, you would probably just as soon skip growing up and start right out as a mature person doing all the things adults get to do. But it just doesn't work that way. God didn't plan it that way. Growing up is something we have to do over a period of time. As we grow, we can do more and more things that we couldn't do when we were first born. That's true physically, psychologically and spiritually. Trying to take short cuts and do things before we've grown enough to do them can get us into heaps of trouble. Imagine what would happen to that sixth-grader if he did actually get hold of a Dallas Cowboy uniform and sneak into a game with those fast, mean 275-pound professional athletes! He would be much wiser to give himself time to mature.

Maturing, growing up, doesn't have to be a painful or frightening process, though. On the contrary, it should be a fun experience, an exciting adventure. It will be that if you look on it as a part of life, something worth doing and enjoying for its own sake. The mistake a lot of young people make is to believe that "life" starts at age eighteen or twenty-one or when they get out of high school or when they graduate from college. What you need to realize, young person, is that you're living life right now. Growing up is part of your life— one of the best parts. By the time you're out of high school or college, you'll have lived about one-fourth of your life. Live as you grow, young person. Let growing up be the vibrant, fulfilling part of your life that God meant it to be.

And, if you learn the joys of growing while you are young, you'll discover one of the greatest truths of the Christian life. That truth is that the thrill and joy of growing, in the spiritual sense, continues all through life.

THREE
THE RIGHT SELF-IMAGE

One of the world's favorite games is that of role playing.
One kind of role playing takes place in school. It's a useful
tool for teaching and illustrating a point. But that's not the
kind of role playing I'm talking about. I'm talking about the
role playing that people do in their everyday lives. The world
establishes certain ideas as to what a man should be like, or
what a woman should be like, and men and women go
through their lives trying to pattern their behavior after those
ideas. They try to act out the roles that the culture of this
world has given them to play.

As a result of role playing, men and women, boys and girls,
have developed a lot of erroneous ideas as to who they are and
how they are supposed to act. The world depicts a man as a
big, muscular bully who lives hard, plays rough, can't cry, and
would rather be shot than do a household chore like sweeping
the floor or washing dishes. The male is also supposed to be a
lady killer—a Casanova. He's supposed to be so tall, dark, and
handsome that the pretty girls swoon when he walks into the
room. In the same way that an Indian warrior was expected to
collect enemy scalps to prove his manhood, the male in our
society is expected to "make out" with as many girls as
possible to validate his masculinity. Girls have their roles to
live up to, also. They're supposed to cry easily, to be soft and
sentimental, scatterbrained and a little dumb, coy, fickle and

seductive. When they grow up to be women, they are supposed to take care of the household chores, raise the kids, and do the churchgoing.

In modern times, with so many women working outside the home and with the feminist movement demanding recognition for women's economic and political rights, these traditional roles are changing. As a result, the world is transmitting a garbled message to modern young people concerning the roles they should be playing. This is causing a great deal of confusion and frustration for boys and girls, and for men and women as well. Because of this confusion, the so-called identity problem, the question of "who am I?" is one of the most troubling social problems of the day.

God didn't mean for us to turn to the world to get our ideas about who we are and what it means to be a man or a woman. He meant for us to get those ideas from him, through his Word. When we let God tell us who we are and who we're becoming, we have a true picture of ourselves. We understand why we're the way we are. We recognize what God is doing to change and develop us. And we know what he wants us to be like when he has finished his work with us.

Having a distorted image of yourself or failing to realize your worth in the eyes of God can get you into all manner of trouble. It can undermine your ability to live by faith in God. If you have a negative attitude about yourself, you may look in the mirror and say, "If that's an example of God's creativity and love, then I want no part of it." A negative self-image can also cause you to resent authority. You may feel cheated. The bitterness you feel over the way you are or the circumstances of your life can cause you to rebel against parents, teachers, civil authorities, employers, etc. Most important of all, so far as dating and marriage are concerned, a bad self-image can hinder your ability to form close relationships of any kind with other people. It tends to prevent you from responding to others as you should. Feeling bitter about yourself, you won't be sensitive to their desires and needs. You will be preoccupied with trying to win their approval and acceptance, rather than serving them and meeting their needs. But people have a way of sensing self-rejection. When they realize that you don't accept yourself, they also tend not to accept you. So a negative self-image works two ways to frustrate you in dating and marriage. It hinders you in getting psychologically and spiritually close to others and it hinders them from getting close to you.

How can you be sure to get a correct image of yourself? Basically, you do so by taking God's word for the value of your life—your appearance, your abilities, the circumstances in which you live—rather than the values other people or you yourself place on your life.

GOD MADE YOU

The first step in getting an accurate image of yourself and your worth is to realize that God made you as you are. Psalm 139:13-16 (TLB) says:

"You made all the delicate, inner parts of my body, and knit them together in my mother's womb. Thank you for making me so wonderfully complex! It is amazing to think about. Your workmanship is marvelous—and how well I know it. You were there while I was being formed in utter seclusion! You saw me before I was born and scheduled each day of my life before I began to breathe. Every day was recorded in your Book!"

You see, God made you as you are—for his purposes. He placed you in the circumstances in which you find yourself— for his purposes. What are his purposes? The overall purpose of your life, remember, is to have fellowship with God and to glorify him in fellowship with other Christians. Beneath the umbrella of these general purposes, though, God has specific purposes for your life. These specific purposes involve the details of your physical and psychological makeup and the circumstances in which you live. God will reveal to you just what these specific purposes are as you need to know them in the course of your life. He will, that is, if you accept the way he has made you and rejoice in it, trusting him to use you for whatever his purposes may be.

You say, "Well, I'm too tall," or, "I'm too short." Too tall for what? Too short for what? Too tall to accomplish some-

thing you want to do out of your own self-will, or too
tall to accomplish what God designed for you? Too short to do
what your associates in the world expect of you, or too short to
do what God expects of you?

Do you see how looking at yourself as a creation of God, for
his purpose, puts a whole new light on your life and its
worth? Looking at your life as a product of God's handiwork,
you'll find it's almost impossible to think of any characteristic
you may have as a "deficiency." You may be deficient in the
eyes of the spiritually blind people around you, but you can
rejoice in it. Why? Because you know that God put that
characteristic in you for some purpose of his own, and you
know that God will fulfill that purpose in some wonderful
way if you will just trust yourself to him.

GOD IS STILL MAKING YOU

The second step in developing a true self-image is to realize that
God isn't through with his "creation" of you yet. His work
will continue throughout your life. "For we are his
workmanship, created in Christ Jesus unto good works, which
God hath before ordained that we should walk in them" (Eph.
2:10).

This tells you that God has set you aside for certain tasks
and that through the work he has for you, he will mold and
shape you as you go through life. Even greater assurance of
this important truth is found in Philippians 1:6: "Being
confident of this very thing, that he which hath begun a good
work in you will perform it [continue to do it] until the day of
Jesus Christ."

The goal of God's work in you is to have you bear the
image of his Son, Jesus Christ, in all that you are and do.
Romans 8:29: "For whom he did foreknow, he also did
predestinate to be conformed to the image of his Son . . . " If
there are any characteristics in your life that God can't use (and
there are many in all of our lives), don't worry about them.
God will work in us and through us to remove what he
doesn't want and to replace it with what he does want. Just as
Michelangelo created a beautiful sculpture from a stone by
chipping away everything that did not resemble an angel, so

God can make something beautiful of your life by chipping away everything that doesn't resemble Jesus Christ.

GOD MADE YOU UNIQUE

A third step in acquiring an accurate self-image is to realize that you are unique, and that God doesn't want you comparing the way he has made you with the way he has made any other person. In 2 Corinthians 10:12, Paul warns Christians: "For we dare not make ourselves of the number, or compare ourselves with some that commend themselves: but they . . . comparing themselves among themselves, are not wise."

God made you with specific purposes in mind. He made others with other purposes in mind. Not all boys were meant to grow up to be great athletes, any more than all were meant to be concert pianists. Not all girls were meant to be models, actresses, or scientists. Comparing yourself to someone designed for a different purpose could lead to unnecessary feelings of inferiority.

A sports reporter was interviewing an outstanding professional football player who was known to be unhappy with his lot and considering retiring from the game. The reporter, obviously envying the physical prowess of the football player, asked, "Why would someone of your ability want to quit football?" The athlete startled the reporter by answering, "Because I've always wanted to do what you're doing."

GOD RISKS HIS REPUTATION ON YOU

A fourth step you can take to secure a positive self-image is to consider the fact that God stakes his reputation on you. Psalm 23 expresses this thought: "He leadeth me in the paths of righteousness *for his name's sake.*" The theme is stated again in Psalm 31:3: "For thou art my rock and my fortress; therefore *for thy name's sake* lead me, and guide me."

God is risking his good name in dealing with you. If you don't turn out well, it will give the world occasion to mock and deride him. For that reason, if you genuinely surrender your life to his workmanship, you can rest assured he won't make any mistakes in molding and shaping your life. He will make you in such a way that you honor and bring glory to his name.

THANK GOD

Finally, you will be well on your way to securing a good image of yourself if you genuinely thank God for making you just as you are and for the work he has done in you thus far.

To bring yourself to do this honestly, you may need to review and ponder the points we have covered, realizing:

—That God has made you as you are for a purpose.

—That God has not finished his work on you until he has made you as he wants you to be.

—That you must not compare your characteristics with others, because God has made each of us for different purposes.

—That God's reputation is at stake; therefore, he will take great pains with his workmanship on you.

After meditating on these truths, you should be able to thank God even for the traits that you have considered "defects," knowing that God intends to use everything about you in some way for your joy and for his glory.

When you have come to know yourself in this way, and realize your worth in the eyes of God, you won't be trapped into the world's role playing game. You won't be trying to act a part in life. You'll be able to be yourself, because you'll know who you are and what God wants you to become. You'll see the patterns of the man or woman God wants you to be in his Holy Word.

Then you will have accomplished an important part of your preparation for dating and marriage. For you'll have acquired an accurate concept of yourself and you will feel good about yourself, knowing that you're being designed and polished for God's purposes. Feeling good about yourself will help you feel good toward others. It will also help others feel good toward you.

These are not principles from a psychology textbook. They're straight from the Scriptures. Jesus listed as the second greatest commandment, "Thou shalt love thy neighbor as thyself." A most important part of that commandment is the word "thyself." God expects us to love ourselves. Only if we love ourselves will we be able to love others—and that includes the marriage partner. But we can't love ourselves unless we realize that we're God's workmanship, that we're important, precious to him, and that he has made us—and is making us— for a purpose.

To love yourself is to know yourself—through the eyes of God. And to love yourself is to be able to love others with the godly kind of love on which stable, fulfilling marriages and homes are built.

FOUR
THE RIGHT WAY

Joan came home from her date with tears streaming down her beautiful young face. Her mother had been waiting up for her. Joan had told her she would be home before midnight. It was now after one o'clock in the morning. "What's the matter, sweetheart?" Joan's mother asked when she saw that her daughter was crying. "Did something go wrong?"

"Everything went wrong," Joan sobbed. "Jack was so crude. He just treated me awful. All he wanted to do was make out. I'm so disgusted I never want to go on a date again."

That can be a crushing experience for a nice teenage girl, raised in a Christian home. The girl has been dying to date the boy for a long time. Finally, the invitation comes. Then the big night rolls around, and there she is, getting into the car with the boy she has been wanting to go out with. She can't believe such a wonderful thing is happening to her—and then to have it all shattered in a nightmare of selfish disrespect.

What goes wrong in cases like this? I'm convinced that what goes wrong, basically, is that the young persons—and perhaps the parents, too—don't have the right concept of the purpose of dating and how to go about dating.

The world plants completely erroneous ideas about dating in the minds of many young people. The world tells the boy that dating is the way to get what he wants from a girl. And in case he doesn't know what he wants, the world tells him that, too.

It tells him he wants sex. It tells him that's all girls are really for—to have sex with. The world beams a phony message to girls about dating, too. It tells them that dating is the way to have a good time. To have that good time, the girl is told, she has to get everything out of the boy that she can. She has to lure him into taking her to the really neat places, buying her nice things, and spending a lot of money on her. If she has to turn on her sexual charms to get him to show her a big time, so what? That's what makes the world go around.

Those lies that the world tells boys and girls are responsible for many problems that are tearing homes apart faster than they can be put together in this country today.

The true purpose of dating is not for the boy to get all the sex he can, and it's not for the girl to exploit the boy to have a good time. Believing those lies, and acting on them, brings only disillusionment, disappointment, and bitterness.

The true purpose of dating is (1) to learn how to get to know persons of the opposite sex and (2) to get to know one certain person of the opposite sex in a special way that prepares you for engagement and marriage.

Please don't misunderstand. I'm not saying that dating shouldn't be fun. It should be—and it is, when done properly. It can be great fun. But the good time is a by-product of a most important learning process, one that determines to a great extent the attitudes and behavior that you will take into your marriage and your home in the future. A girl should never accept a date with a boy who she thinks, judging from what she already knows about him, would not contribute in a positive way to this vital educational process. A boy should not ask a girl for a date unless he feels sure she is someone who will help him learn to know girls in the right way, and perhaps someone whom he might wish to get to know intimately.

At this point, though, it's vital that you understand the proper meaning of that word "intimate." It doesn't mean what the world says it means, what the devil says it means. The world and Satan try to tell you that you can't be intimate with someone unless you have sex with that person. But that's not what God means when he talks about intimacy.

When God talks about intimacy, he refers to genuine fellowship. In the Scriptures, he says that he wants to be intimate in his fellowship with those who believe in him. He wants to be to his church as a man is to a woman in marriage, he says. He means that he wants to be joined in spirit and soul to those who love him. That's also the way in which God wants young people to become intimate in dating. He specifically forbids them to become intimate in a physical sense.

The world has come up with a popular term for that kind of intimacy. It's called "premarital sex." But God calls it fornication. Sex apart from marriage is fornication, and God detests it. In Acts 15:20 he warns young people to "abstain from fornication." In 1 Corinthians 5:1, through the Apostle Paul, he shames a group of Christians because "there is fornication among you." In Ephesians 5:3, he admonishes Christians: "fornication . . . let it not once be named among you." In Revelation 14:8, he cites fornication in figurative language as a symbol of the wantonness that incurs his terrible wrath.

Why does God hate fornication so much? Because it's a device of the Devil to lure men and women and young people from serving God to serving Satan. "The body is not for fornication, but for the Lord," God says (1 Cor. 6:13). Sexual activity involves not just the body but the total person. God designed your total personality to serve him. If you give your body over to fornication, you deprive God of the glory he is entitled to receive from your life. You disrupt his plan for you. You rob not only God but also yourself, because the Bible says that persons who engage in fornication are never the same (Prov. 6-7). Their personalities are forever changed. This does not mean that they can't be forgiven. God does forgive those who repent and turn to him and he can take a shattered life and make something beautiful of it. But it can never be the life it could have been without that awful scar inflicted by the sin of fornication.

How can premarital sex—fornication—be so lastingly harmful? Because it destroys the order of things as God planned it. God ordained a certain procedure for a man and

woman to follow in getting to know each other intimately
and Satan's program demolishes the order. Trying to put
together a healthy, fulfilling relationship by the Devil's plan is
like trying to build cars with the parts all arranged in the
wrong places on the assembly line.

God's order calls for man and woman to become united first
in spirit, then in soul, and finally in body. These three
different types of intimacy need to be carefully defined and
understood.

SPIRITUAL INTIMACY

In spiritual intimacy, the object is for the man and woman to
get to know each other so that they are able to share freely
with each other the working of God in their lives. That being
the goal, it's absolutely essential that both be Christians. Two
nonbelievers can't share about how God is dealing with them,
because they can't know or understand such dealings. That
understanding comes only when the Holy Spirit comes to
dwell in the believer and reveal spiritual truths to him.
Spiritual sharing can't take place if one is a Christian and the
other is not. The non-Christian can't understand spiritual
things (1 Cor. 2:14)

You may be thinking, "Shouldn't Christians date non-
Christians to try to lead them to Christ?" No. Christians
should witness to non-Christians, of course, but not in the
dating situation. And they should be careful about dating
persons whom they have won to the Lord, because
nonbelievers have been known to make false professions of faith
just to get the opportunity to date a certain Christian.

Christians should date Christians, and by that I mean Bible-
believing, praying Christians who show evidence of spiritual
growth in their lives. When two growing, maturing Christians
date, the foundation exists for building genuine spiritual
oneness. If that common foundation of Christian experience is
lacking, the stage is set for unhappiness and probably for
serious trouble later on in the relationship.

Dating is the phase of life in which you can learn how to
get to know people of the opposite sex intimately on the spiri-

tual level. You can share openly and completely with them concerning how Christ saved you and how he is working in you and through you to make your life what he wants it to be. It can be a time in which you and your date learn about each other and God together, grow in your commitment to him and participate in witnessing and Christian service as a team. You can become spiritually intimate with more than one person with no harm to anyone concerned. In fact, all involved should benefit from it. Ultimately, you may become deeply intimate with a certain person of the opposite sex, and that relationship could lead to the next step in God's order of things.

MENTAL AND EMOTIONAL INTIMACY

This is the next step—intimacy of soul. The Bible tells us that the soul involves three aspects of the human personality: the intellect, the emotions, and the will. In developing soul oneness, persons of the opposite sex must first have achieved spiritual oneness. Without that, they lack a proper foundation for this next stage of intimacy. Soul oneness entails planning together for a future that the man and woman intend to share. It involves learning to share their deepest likes and dislikes as they contemplate living and working together.

The focus of the relationship of the couple at this stage of intimacy is upon the time when these plans for a shared life of intimacy can be fulfilled. Both partners look forward with great excitement and expectation toward this time.

Soul intimacy is achieved during the period known as engagement, the time span between the couple's making a commitment to live and work together in total oneness and their marriage date.

PHYSICAL INTIMACY

Intimacy at this stage, involving the body and sexual relations, is reserved for marriage in God's order of things. The first two stages of intimacy prepare a couple for this closest and most complete intimacy—physical oneness. Mark 10:7,8: "For this cause shall a man leave his father and mother, and cleave to his wife; and they twain shall be one flesh . . . " That's the mathematics God uses to build homes—one plus one equals one. For God's math to work, though, his rules must be followed just as you have to follow the rules of math to solve an algebraic equation. Disregarding the rules can be as tragic to a couple trying to build a life as disregarding the rules of algebra and trigonometry would be to an engineer designing a missile or a skyscraper.

As I gave the invitation in one of my crusades one night, I noticed a beautiful young girl standing right at the foot of the platform trying to get my attention. She kept holding her hands up toward me and pleading, "I need to talk to you— will you talk to me, please?" Scores of people were streaming out of the stands of the huge football stadium, and I was trying to complete the invitation, so I put her off. "I can't talk to you right now, young lady," I explained, "because all of these people have come to make decisions for Christ and I need to talk to them." But she kept waving at me and calling to me. She kept saying, "I just want to ask you one question."

Finally, I bent down and said, "All right, young lady, but I can only give you a minute. What did you want to ask?"

She said, "Do you believe in abortion?"

I said, "No, I don't." Then, as I looked into the weeping eyes of this beautiful girl—she must have been about fifteen—a lump came in my throat. I asked her, "Young lady, do you need an abortion?"

And she responded with the answer I dreaded to hear. "Yes," she said, "I need an abortion."

That girl's story is one among tens of thousands of real-life tragedies being played out on the stage of modern society because young people are disregarding God's order of things. They're listening to the world. They're listening to the Devil. They're getting a cheap, pornographic picture of what life and sex are all about, and they're paying for it in the cruel currency of anxiety, bitterness, agony, and even death.

For those who know God's order for dating, engagement, and marriage, though, the Lord has prepared riches of challenge, joy, and fulfillment. Now let's examine in more detail the principles of spiritual intimacy through dating. Soul intimacy and physical intimacy will be discussed in greater detail in the chapters on engagement and marriage.

SPIRITUAL ONENESS THROUGH DATING

As I pointed out earlier, the purpose of dating is to develop spiritual intimacy, or oneness, between two persons of the opposite sex. If you have listened to the world and the Devil's "good time" ideas about dating, you're probably saying, "Yuk, what a drag!" But I'm leveling with you, young people, when I say there's nothing that can thrill you and fulfill you like the God-given adventure of growing and maturing spiritually with another person. It's not a good time—it's the best time. It's not fun—it's fantastic!

In developing spiritual intimacy, you're gaining a greater love for God, and you're sharing the joy of seeing another grow in that love. Scripture study and prayer become a joyous adventure. Your heart burns to share Jesus with others, and as you share these things your fellowship with the one you're dating becomes deeper and richer than you could have ever imagined.

Even in this stage of intimacy, though, God has a design that should be carefully observed. The boy should be the spiritual leader. When he marries, the man is responsible for the spiritual leadership of his family. Dating provides opportunity for training in that responsibility. The boy should become accustomed and skilled in spiritual leadership through the dating experience. The girl's responsibility in the dating relationship also foreshadows the responsibility that will be hers when she becomes a wife and mother. She's to be the spiritual challenge and encouragement to her date, just as she will later be the spiritual challenge and encouragement to her husband. By the depth of her love for the Lord and by the standards she sets, the girl inspires the boy to develop spiritually and to provide strong spiritual leadership.

In regard to these responsibilities, though, I have a firm word of warning for both the boy and the girl.

First, the girl is never to take it upon herself to remold a boy's life. That's God's responsibility, not the girl's. Only God can transform the life of an individual. If a girl begins to encroach on God's work, one of two things is likely to happen. She'll either cause such resentment in the boy that he'll be turned off completely to her or they will have a bitter, unhappy pairing in which the boy never fulfills his

responsibility as spiritual leader and the girl becomes a nag
and scold rather than an encouragement.

Now for the boy's responsibility. He should remember that
being a leader means precisely that. It means leading, not
pushing or trying to shove the girl out ahead. Leading in the
spiritual sense demands that the boy devote himself to spiritual
growth through Bible study, prayer, and living according to
spiritual principles. He must accept responsibility for the girl's
growth, too.

A common fault of men is to expect their wives to be
spiritually stronger than they are. They should instead attend
to their own spiritual growth and lead their wives to grow
with them. To lead spiritually, a boy must learn to be tactful
and not tyrannical. That means he must follow God's
leadership closely. An individual can be led in spiritual
development only as rapidly as God is able to complete his
work. Trying to lead at your own pace, rather than God's
pace, can cause progress toward spiritual oneness to be
seriously hindered.

To summarize spiritual responsibilities in dating: The boy
should lead spiritually, not lag. He should lead at God's pace,
not push for a pace of his own choosing. The girl should
challenge and encourage, not nag or command. She should
avoid trying to usurp God's responsibility for molding the
character of her date. She should inspire him with her own
love for the Lord and set standards of spiritual maturity for
him to achieve. But she should let the achievement of those
standards be between the boy and God. As one Bible teacher
and counselor has put it: "The girl should put in her order—
then let God fill it."

When a boy fully accepts his responsibility for spiritual
leadership in the dating experience, he lets himself in for one
of the most gratifying encounters life offers. Nothing will goad
you to spiritual growth like the realization that you're
responsible for someone else's spiritual development. You'll get
down to business with your Christianity. You won't be just a
playacting Christian. You'll start to discover spiritual truths
you never dreamed existed. In these discoveries, you'll
experience the joy the Lord intends for all his children to have.
You'll share that joy with your date. Then you'll receive the

double blessing reserved for those who dare to step out in faith to exercise spiritual leadership. You'll know the joy of seeing your date appropriate and benefit from your leadership and the spiritual discoveries you've shared with her.

What about the girl? Is she cheated? Does she get only a single blessing, while he gets a double one? Not on your life. She gets not only the blessing of her own growth but the unspeakable blessing of comfort and security that comes with the knowledge that her date is accepting and fulfilling his responsibility for her spiritual well-being.

How does violating God's order in dating and preparation for future marriage work to destroy spiritual oneness and prevent a happy, fulfilling relationship from being formed? Well, the key element is guilt.

God created you in his image and built into you a sense of what you ought to be and how you ought to develop spiritually. When you depart from the direction he charted for your development, your conscience lets you know about it. If you don't correct your course, you and your conscience—that is, your will and your conscience—begin to struggle against each other. You can't construct any kind of satisfactory relationship with another person when you have a war going on inside yourself. Your guilt rises up and accuses you and puts you down. You frantically try to silence your guilt. This leads to hostilities and other reactions that drive a wedge between you and the person you're dating.

You find it difficult to communicate with your date. You may begin to quarrel. You seem to have less and less in common, instead of more and more as you would in a growing intimacy. You seem to drift farther apart, rather than come closer together.

You may not recognize the problem as guilt—if you're not spiritually mature, you probably won't. The world refuses to recognize guilt. Or if it does, it blames "taboos" and "fundamentalist religious beliefs" for the guilt and tries to tell the guilty that they shouldn't pay any attention to their feelings. The world says "if it feels good do it, and don't let your conscience tell you there's anything wrong with it." But the world lies. You can't throw off the consequences of guilt by trying to disregard guilt feelings. Even if you don't have the feelings—as many who are not saved may not—guilt will do its work in you. Guilt results from being guilty, and if you listen to the world instead of listening to God you're guilty. If you follow the world's order of things rather than God's order, you're guilty. And, if you're guilty, guilt will inevitably take its toll on your life and your relationship with others.

Millions of couples are experiencing trouble and distress in their dating and marriage relationships right now because of guilt resulting from not obeying God. More and more, the guilt arises from premarital sexual relations. But damaging guilt can result even if the problem doesn't progress that far.

A fellow, call him John, had allowed his relationship with the girl he was engaged to marry to develop along physical lines first, rather than nurturing oneness in spirit and in soul. He felt some guilt about it at the time, but he justified it by comparing the relatively "harmless" things they were doing with the much worse things other couples were doing. After marriage, John and his wife began having problems. They couldn't get along. She seemed to resent him.

Finally, during one of their arguments, she let him know why she resented him and couldn't really give herself to him physically. "You dated a lot of other girls before you started going with me, and I know how you acted with me," she said. Then she dropped the bombshell that woke him up to the source of the trouble. She said: "I'll bet you went just as far with some of those girls as you did with me, and maybe a lot farther."

After thinking it over, John realized that his behavior with his wife when they were dating had been similar to the way he had behaved with other girls. He also came to the realization that his guilt had been causing him to behave in a phony way toward his wife, in a way that she knew was not genuine and sincere. He had been trying to buy her affection with things, rather than really giving her his heart. He had been hiding his guilt with religious activities and false intellectualism. All of these things were only making his wife more suspicious of him and destroying communication between them. Having realized the source of the problem, John was able to go to the Lord and get the problem solved and get his marriage put back together.

Before John could do anything constructive, though, he had to realize that he had violated God's plan. He had to acknowledge that guilt had built an impenetrable barrier between his wife and himself, and that their marriage wasn't going to work until that barrier was ripped out.

STANDARDS FOR DATING

If you're a young person just thinking about starting to date, or if you're a parent with a child going into the teens, you should set up a list of standards for dating right now. You should commit them to the Lord and then trust him for the strength to adhere to them in the face of all the pressures the world and the Devil can bring to bear against you. Here are some basic standards worked out by one marriage counselor. These standards are drawn from the Bible, from spiritual principles set forth in the Word of God.

First, you should resolve not to date until the timing is right; that is, until you are old enough. How do you know when you are old enough? Well, your age in years doesn't offer a reliable gauge. Your mental, emotional, and spiritual maturity should be the determining factor. Generally speaking, you can assume you are old enough to date:

—When you realize that the true purpose for dating is to prepare you for engagement and marriage by helping you learn to develop spiritual oneness with a person of the opposite sex. Only when you are truly aware of this purpose will you become aware of both the benefits and the inherent dangers of dating.

—When you have worked out from the Bible a set of standards to live by during dating. You should ask mature, spiritually stable Christians to help you with these standards. Hopefully, these helpers would include your parents. But if they're not strong Christians then you should seek the help of your pastor, Sunday school teacher, or some other spiritually mature person.

—When you can truthfully say to yourself that you have committed yourself to follow these standards, and never to compromise them, no matter what the cost. If it means not being asked out on dates, if it means staying at home, if it means losing a chance to date the boy or girl you've always wanted to date, you stick with your standards. If you are ready to do that, you're ready to date. But there's one more condition.

—When your parents realize that you have achieved the above three levels of maturity and agree with you that you are old enough to date. You can be short-changed in your dating experience and in later life by starting to date without your parents' consent and approval. If your parents doubt that you are old enough or mature enough to date, give them the benefit of that doubt. Work on developing and demonstrating more maturity. If they still balk in giving you permission to date, ask God to open their eyes to your level of maturity. The blessing of your parents is essential to success of anything you do in life—and your ability to derive satisfaction from it. This is no more true of any activity than that of dating.

Now, to continue with the set of dating standards. This is only a good model to work from. It offers sound basic principles. You can build on it, adding greater detail as the Lord leads you to discover the need for other standards.

1. Date Only Christians. This is one of the hardest rules for young Christians to live by. You get all sorts of reasons from the world to go ahead and date non-Christians. And if you don't watch yourself, you'll be coming up with your own reasons for doing so.

"After all, it's only a date—just one little old date." "He (or she) isn't a Christian but he (or she) is still a nice guy (or girl)." "He (or she) is more of a gentleman (or lady) than most of the Christians I know." "He (or she) is just too honest to be a Christian. He (or she) doesn't want to be a hypocrite." "Other than religion, we have a lot of things in common." "I think he (or she) would become a Christian if the right person talked to him (or her). I could witness on our dates." "I told him (or her) I would date only Christians, so he (or she) accepted Christ."

If you hear any of these rationalizations for dating non-Christians coming at you, whether they come from your own mind or someone else's lips, be on guard. You're being lured into a trap.

Non-Christians can be very charming socially. They sometimes seem nicer than Christians because they spend more time and energy developing the social graces. That's all they have going for them. But you can't develop spiritual oneness with someone who isn't spiritual, no matter how nice that person may seem. So, if you date someone who isn't a Christian, you're thwarting your very purpose in dating—developing spiritual oneness.

The idea that a person can be too honest to be a Christian is simply ludicrous. Christ said, "I am . . . the Truth." He reveals truth to those who come to him—truth about themselves, about the world, about others. Christians can be hypocrites, and some are. But no Christian should be a hypocrite and, certainly, no Christian has to be one.

As mentioned earlier in this book, dating just isn't the proper setting for witnessing. Dating is for sharing spiritual experiences, not for leading someone to spiritual birth. Witnessing during dating can lead to distortions in your spiritual development and that of your date, and these distortions can cause trouble later in marriage. The boy should be developing spiritual leadership, remember, and the girl should be practicing fulfilling her responsibility for setting standards and for encouraging her date to grow and fulfill those standards. That's what dating is for. Witnessing on dates can seriously upset these functions and purposes.

You should be leery of dating a boy (or girl) you have witnessed to and led to Christ before the invitation to date. This is especially true if you have told this person or he or she has heard from others, that you will date only Christians. In this case, the boy or girl may not have had a genuine salvation experience. He or she may simply be paying lip service to Christianity to get a date with you. Even if the commitment to Christ is sincere, however, you should give the person time to grow spiritually before dating him (or her). Then, when you do date the new Christian, it can be a sharing situation, rather than one instructing or pushing the other. Also, if the profession of faith was not genuine, time will reveal the falseness of it.

For dating to fulfill its purpose, the boy and girl should both be Christians.

2. *Build Your Dating Around God's Purpose.* You may think after you've had a date or two that this person you're dating is

just shy when it comes to discussing religious things. Just remember this: No Christian who loves the Lord and is feasting on God's Word and engaged in a vital prayer life and a real walk with the Lord is going to be tongue-tied about it. He'll be talking his head off about it. All he'll want to do will be share what God's doing in his life. If someone seems shy about his faith, it means one of two things. It either means he doesn't have any faith or else he's terribly immature in his faith. You would be wise to proceed with caution in dating anyone who is that shy.

Or, it may seem after you've been out on a few dates with this boy or girl that "it just never seems to be the right time to talk about God or spiritual things." Boys, since it's your responsibility to provide spiritual leadership, you're the ones who may encounter this problem. You may try to lead the conversation to spiritual things and find her always changing the subject or suggesting, "Oh, come on, let's go to a movie," or, "Let's take in a concert and have some fun."

If she's always trying to keep you away from spiritual things, it's time to ask yourself what's going on. She's either spiritually unborn or she's spiritually immature.

Girls can run into the same problem in their dating role. They should let the boy lead, but if he never leads to spiritual things he should be dropped. If he's a Christian, it may be that he needs the Lord to work more maturity into his life before he is ready for you to date.

You can also get the idea from the world that your date might suspect you're a religious fanatic if you want to talk about the Lord and spiritual growth. If the boy or girl you're dating thinks that, then he or she is not spiritually mature enough for you to date. A spiritually mature person will understand and share your desire to discuss spiritual matters. You don't have to worry about what he or she will think of you. If your date doesn't understand you, then it may be a signal from God warning you to stay away from that person.

Keep in mind God's purpose for you in dating. Don't let your date, or anyone else, pull you off course.

3. Avoid Physical Involvement. You've already learned the dangers of becoming physically involved. The main danger is that it can lead to premarital sex and its awful aftermath in later years. Short of that, it can still produce guilt feelings that make a true oneness virtually impossible to achieve.

Another problem resulting from physical involvement, however, is one not mentioned before in this book. It's the problem of defrauding.

To defraud sexually means simply to arouse desires in another person that you can't fulfill. Or, I should say, desires that you can't fulfill without violating God's order of things, without breaking God's moral law.

You can defraud your date in this way with even the slightest, seemingly most harmless physical involvement. You can do so even by the way you talk, dress, or behave.

When a boy or girl is being defrauded—when desires are being aroused that can't be properly met in the dating situation—the result will be frustration, resentment and bitterness. The world justifies defrauding techniques on the grounds that "dating standards are different now" or that you have to do something to "express your feelings." If a boy is trying to arouse sexual desire in a girl, she may try to excuse him by saying, "I don't like for him to behave this way but all boys are like this." Or, "I should break up with him but I don't want to hurt his feelings."

Such justifications are from the Devil. Don't listen to them. Stick to your dating standards. Remember your dating purpose. It would be far better for you to lose out with this boy or girl than to violate God's plan and try to build a relationship on the wrong kind of foundation.

4. Be Sure Both Are in Harmony at Home. If you've got problems at home, get them straightened out before you start dating. If you're interested in someone who has problems at home, don't go out with him or her until those problems are resolved. Problems in one relationship have a way of being transmitted to other relationships. Problems in the home of one or the other dating partner will crop up in some form, sooner or later, in the dating situation or in the marriage that follows.

Your girl may tell you, "You're the only one I can talk to." If so, a good question for you to ask is, "Why?" If she can't get along with her parents, she may have some basic personality flaws that ultimately will make it impossible for you to get along with her.

Or your fellow may say, "You're the only one who understands me." You should ask, "Why are you so hard to understand?" Maybe it's because he wants his own way so badly that nobody can stand him, much less *under*stand him. You should encourage him to work out those problems at home. When harmony has been established there, he can come back and see if you would care to date him.

And moving out of the home is not the answer. That's the solution more and more young people are turning to today. They can't get along with their parents. So instead of trying to get to the roots of the problems and get them straightened out, they just pack up and leave. They get an apartment with other young people.

But they haven't solved their problems; they've only run from them. They haven't learned how to face the challenge of working out the difficulties that can arise in close interpersonal relationships. They haven't learned to cope.

If a boy or girl says to you, in asking you to date: "I couldn't get along with my parents but I've moved out now and everything's going to be OK," your comeback should be: "Don't tell me your troubles until you've solved them." You're going to have enough of a challenge working out the rough spots between you and the one you date without having to deal with the problems he or she brings from home.

5. *Yield All Rights to God.* There may not seem to be any Christians to date at your school or in your circle of friends.. Or that may not be the problem. The problem may be that none of the Christians you know are interested in you. In either case, there's a verse in Psalms that you should claim and cling to. "Wait on the Lord," it says, "be of good courage, and he shall strengthen thine heart: wait, I say, on the Lord" (Psa. 27:14).

Wait on the Lord, and he will bring into your life the boy or girl he wants for you. Or it may be that he has another purpose for you rather than dating and becoming engaged and married. You must be willing to wait for him to reveal his will to you, whatever it may be. But before he will reveal his will, you've got to be willing to do it.

This much is certain: God's basic will is for you to yield your life completely to him. Once you've done that, you have given God the freedom to do in your life what he otherwise cannot do, whether that is to bring you together with a girl (or boy) or to prepare you for a life of service to him as a single. You can make serious mistakes by directing your own life. You can't go wrong by letting God do it.

Having read to this point, you may be saying, "I give up; my dating patterns are so far wrong that I can never straighten them out. I'm too far gone."

Not so. No matter how far you've strayed from God's perfect order in your dating, or even in your marriage, he can restore you. God's in the business of putting together the pieces, of mending things that have been broken, of remaking vessels that were marred in the mold. If that weren't so, there would be no Christianity. God has nothing perfect to work with. He takes things just as they are, right where they are, and works in them and through them to make them perfect.

Remember, the Scriptures say, "But God commendeth his love toward us, in that, while we were yet sinners, Christ died for us" (Rom. 5:8). God didn't wait for sinners to clean up their lives before sending Christ to die for them. He knew that wouldn't work. He sent Christ to die while all were still sinners. Not one finger had been lifted by anyone to rid himself of sin. All were sinning and falling short of the glory God intended for them. (See Romans 3:23.) And, when Christ did appear, they despised and rejected him. (See John 1:11.) Talk about too far gone! The world was so far gone when Christ came that they didn't even want to be saved. But it was while they remained in that despicable state that Christ laid down his life for them on the cross.

However, only those who believed in him and turned to him could be saved (see John 1:12), and that's how it is with you today. If you have not followed God's plan in your dating life, and you now see where you've gone wrong, God can help you get your life straightened out. But he can do so only when you turn to him and put your life in his hands.

In the language of the Bible, that's called repenting. It simply means turning from doing things your own way and letting God do them his way.

That may mean breaking off a relationship for a time—maybe permanently. If that's what it takes to get on the right path and follow God's plan for dating, then you would be far better off to break up than to go on the way you are and hope things will get better. They won't get better. They'll get worse. And they'll get worse fast now that you know you're doing wrong and your conscience will be working in full force.

When they launch a missile at Cape Canaveral and it goes off course, they push a button and destroy it instantly. They know that once a missile has strayed from its course there's no longer any hope for it. It won't straighten itself out. From that point, things can only go from bad to worse. Innocent people could be hurt or killed.

That's how it is with a dating relationship that has not followed God's compass heading. Stop it—right there. Talk your new dating standards over with your date and see if he (or she) will agree to part for a time, work on spiritual growth independently, and then perhaps come back together. Then you can attempt, in the power of God, to get started on the right foot, working toward spiritual oneness and leaving off physical involvement. That will be humanly impossible to do, and you would do well to realize this at the outset. If you're able to do this, it will be because of the power of God in both of your lives. That's the only way it can be done. If you try it and you see it's not going to work, then it's probably not God's will for this relationship to continue. Like the flight of the errant missile, you should break it off before it does irreparable damage. Some of the damage could be to persons other than yourselves, innocent bystanders— perhaps the children of an unhappy marriage that could grow out of your relationship.

The anatomy of almost every broken marriage reads like a chain reaction of events beginning with the date life of one or both marriage partners and culminating in a family-shattering mushroom of emotional explosion. If a boy and girl disregard God's order in dating, their characters develop along certain lines, step by step, and events in their lives show the progress of that development.

For the boy, the first wrong step is to begin dating a girl solely because of her physical attraction to him. Now, that isn't to say that physical attraction should play no part in causing a boy to want to date a girl. I'm only saying that this should not be the principal motivation. Christian boys will find many girls physically cute and alluring whom they shouldn't date and won't want to date, if they remember that the basic purpose for dating is to develop spiritual oneness. If a boy dates purely for physical reasons, he's not thinking about helping another person to grow spiritually. He's thinking only about getting his sex drives satisfied at someone else's expense. He's approaching dating from a strictly selfish point of view. The Bible calls this lasciviousness.

A girl can approach dating from a lascivious motive, too. Instead of thinking about God's purpose and desiring to contribute to a boy's spiritual development, she simply wants to hook a cute boy to make other girls jealous. Or she can want to catch someone who will take her to the most expensive places and show her a good time. If these are her motives, she concentrates on making herself physically alluring. She wears clothing that accentuates her sexual attributes and talks and behaves in a suggestive, seductive way.

The outcome of a dating experience motivated by lasciviousness will inevitably be physical intimacy of some degree. In today's society, which actually encourages such things, that intimacy probably will go all the way to premarital sex.

Whether or not the physical intimacy progresses to sexual relations, it sets up a chain of mental and emotional events in both the boy and the girl.

The boy develops an erroneous sense of values, a faulty system of moral standards. He feels that he has to prove his love, but the only way he knows to go about it is with physical intimacy. He equates sex with love. Instead of being an expression of love, as God intended it, sex becomes an evidence or a proof of love. This applies pressure on the boy to perform sexually in order to hold the girl's affection. It also generates an increased desire for sexual excitement in order to satisfy his physical craving.

The girl experiences insecurity in this type of relationship. She becomes more concerned with keeping the boy interested in her than with maintaining her moral standards. Gradually, she gives in to his seemingly uncontrollable desire to possess her physically.

This is how so many couples get involved in premarital sex. The girl, sensing that physical intimacy is the only way to hold the boy, goes farther and farther in that intimacy. She has guilt feelings, but she suppresses them, because attracting and keeping the boy has become her consuming ambition in life. At the same time, though, the physical involvement immediately begins to plant seeds of distrust in the girl. She asks herself, "Is he wanting to do the same thing with other girls? Am I as attractive to him as other girls? How long will it be before he sees another girl he thinks more attractive and starts doing these things with her?"

Meanwhile, preoccupied with physical involvement, both the boy and the girl try in various ways to rationalize their behavior. They try to justify what they're doing and make excuses for it. The world now has given them a ready-made justification: "Everybody's doing it." In the new world of relative morals, things are judged right and wrong according to what percentage of the population is doing them. If the public opinion polls show that 57 percent of teenagers are having premarital sex, that becomes justification for everybody to do it.

Sexual activity tends to separate the couple from others, however. They tend to withdraw from the groups they have been associating with and get off to themselves. But, to their surprise, they find that their physical involvement also separates them from each other. Neither can discover the other's real self. They thought their physical involvement, their petting and sex, would bring them together. Instead, they seem farther apart. They find themselves arguing, breaking up, trying to make up again, going through one emotional upheaval after another. In many cases, if not in dating then at some time after marriage, the frustrations arising out of physical intimacy and its failure to provide real closeness can lead to experimentation with deviant forms of sexual relations. That can only produce further trauma and division.

The pattern for destruction having been set in dating, it continues and intensifies in marriage.

The husband views marriage as an acceptable way to meet his needs for physical sex. Still equating sex with love, he tells his wife of his love for her only when he wants sexual gratification. Naturally, she begins to question his love in her heart. She believes that the only reason he loves her is for what he can get from her—and in that she's right. She may become sexually frigid. Short of that, she probably will not be fully satisfied sexually, and she'll be afraid that he isn't either. She becomes hypersensitive. The "little things" he does or doesn't do upset her out of proportion to their importance. She reads everything as a sign that he doesn't love her.

Each begins to try to change the other. She tries to get him to show love for her in ways other than sex. He tries to get her to become more sexually fulfilling to him. As these efforts fail, they drift further apart. They become like strangers to each other.

The disintegration of the relationship continues as the problems intensify and become more complex. He grows angry because her coolness threatens the fulfillment of his sexual desires. He becomes more argumentative, more demanding. She feels a sense of guilt in realizing she is not fulfilling his expectations of her as a wife. This causes her to withdraw into brooding and worrying. Losing her self-confidence, she becomes domineering and contentious. These are psychological devices she uses, without realizing what is happening, to cover up her feelings of inferiority and inadequacy. But these devices, like the ones her husband is using on his side of the relationship, only work to exacerbate the problems between them.

At this point, he may become concerned about the need to do something to rekindle her affections for him. After all, her growing aloofness and moodiness is seriously interfering with his sex life. Out of selfish motives, he may begin to try to win her back by lavishing material things on her—buying her gifts, a new car, a new home, furniture. It's amazing the lengths to which a husband may go in trying to buy affection. Unless he is wealthy, though, this will only add financial distress to all the other problems.

The wife begins to become resigned to the fact that her marriage is going to be unhappy. In a reaction to her guilt feelings, she may even feel that God is punishing her for not adhering to her moral standards or for not being as submissive to her husband as she should be. Seeking a substitute for her husband's love, which she now feels she can never know again, she focuses love on her children, friends or material possessions.

Her husband reacts by beginning to think he may have married the wrong woman. This leads to thoughts of who the right woman might be. Trying to picture that "right woman," he begins to look around and search for her in the women with whom he comes in contact on the job or in other places on his daily routine. In the case of many men, this leads to unfaithfulness. The result can be almost instant dissolution of the marriage when the wife discovers the unfaithfulness.

There's another course, equally destructive, that can be taken at this juncture. The husband may simply give up on his relationship with his wife and start trying to find fulfillment in his job or profession. He can become a "workaholic," a compulsive worker who spends all his time with his occupation and none with his wife and family.

In this stage of the deteriorating marriage, the wife may simply give up on the marriage, too. She may become insensitive to the interests and feelings of others, even her own children. She may become condemning, hypercritical of others, suspicious of other people and their motives, especially of her husband. If she suspects her husband of infidelity, she may become distrustful of all people. To compensate for her lack of fulfillment in the marriage and the home, she may become a busybody and a gossip. Or, increasingly in modern society, she seeks affairs with other men, more as a means to get even with her husband or recapture his attention than to find sexual gratification.

So you see the disastrous course of events that develops when God's plan is disregarded. This is the pattern seen in multitudes of marriages today. It's the pattern that is filling the divorce courts—causing divorces to outnumber marriages each year in most of the nation's large metropolitan areas.

How important it is to follow God's order—spiritual oneness first, then oneness of soul, then physical oneness after marriage!

A newspaper story published as this was written told the heartbreaking story of two celebrities—you would recognize their names if I gave them—whose marriage was on the rocks. The woman was quoted as saying: "I want nothing more than

for us to be a family but the problem, I think, is the pressure
in his life." She went on to say that he was "into adoration,"
wanting to be idolized by others and being plunged into
despondency when criticized. She said he had told her: "You're
the most beautiful woman I know, both inside and outside,
but I need to be free."

Without knowing it, these two were giving us a real-life
example of a marriage entered into without observing God's
order of things. The marrige shows much evidence of
selfishness, of intent to fulfill personal desires rather than to
contribute to the life of another person and develop that other
person's qualities. It shows no signs of oneness of soul, in
which goals and objectives and purposes were shared and
commitments were made, one to the other, long before the
marrige vows were spoken.

In fact, like so many marriages, this was not really a marriage
to begin with. It was just an attempt by two individuals to live
together and come together at the physical level. There was no
foundation of shared spiritual salvation, shared commitment to
serve God and each other, shared motives or shared goals. The
only thing shared was a bedroom. Such an arrangement, so
lacking in the foundations of oneness ordained by God, didn't
have a chance. It was doomed to failure before the preacher
or justice of the peace ever said, "You may kiss the bride."

If you are already married and realize that the entire basis of
your marriage is wrong, you can't break it off. You need to
work with God's help within the marriage to shift it onto the
proper spiritual foundation. Proceed with great tact and
caution in approaching your mate on this matter. He or she
may not be spiritually mature enough to understand the nature
of the problem. The relationship may have deteriorated to the
point that communication on any level is all but impossible.

However, I've seen God put back together some marriages
that everybody had given up on—the marriage partners, the
children, marriage counselors, and everyone who knew
anything about them. God can work miracles when people let
him.

The first thing you must do, whether you're a teenager who
realizes God's principles are not being followed in dating or a
partner in a marriage that's falling apart, is to surrender your

life completely to the will of God. You must be willing to let him have his way in your life, and follow his principles and standards in your relationship, regardless of what the cost may seem to be.

Notice, I said, regardless of what the cost may *seem* to be. The Devil sometimes makes the cost seem much more than it really is. It can be high, however. But it's a bargain compared to the cost of going on doing things the wrong way.

If you know you're not in the center of God's will, stop right where you are, ask his forgiveness and receive his cleansing, then yield your life totally to him. Whatever it's like now, he can make something beautiful of it.

Until now, I haven't mentioned love in connection with dating, and you're probably saying, "Hold it a second! Where does love come in?"

Well, love definitely enters into this picture, but there's one thing we need to get straight before we discuss it any further. Not everything that people call by the name of love is really love. Some people use the term "making love" when they're talking about having premarital sex. But fornication is not love. Adultery is not love. Sex is not love.

The Greek language has more than one word for love. Each describes a different kind of love. One of those words gives our English language the term "erotic." That's the kind of love people experience when they have premarital sex—erotic love. It really isn't love—it's passion, a craving to fulfill a sensual desire.

The Greek word *agape*—pronounced ah-GAH-pay—is the word that stands for the highest order of love. It's the word the Bible uses in John 3:16 to say that "God so loved the world." It's the word Jesus used in saying, "A new commandment I give unto you, That ye love one another; as I have loved you, that ye also love one another." (John 13:34) Agape is Godlike love, the kind of love that never fails no matter what tragic events develop, no matter what devastating circumstances assail it. When the Apostle Paul said, "And now abideth faith, hope, love, these three; but the greatest of these is love," he used the word agape. That's real love

Agape love has nothing to do with physical attraction. " . for the Lord seeth not as man seeth; for man looketh on the outward appearance, but the Lord looketh on the heart" (1 Sam. 16:7). God's love looks for an attractiveness that comes from within the person, not for the good looks that present themselves externally. The Devil can use any kind of external appearance—rugged, manly, handsome; beautiful, feminine, dainty—to deceive you and draw you to the wrong person, or a person who will be wrong for you. True love looks for attractiveness that emanates from the heart. The heart, in Scripture, refers to the personality. It includes the mind, will, and emotions of the person. It has to do with who a person is, rather than what he or she looks like.

That's a most important concept, for it stands to reason that two people must know each other before they can love each other with that kind of love. You hear the phrase "love at first sight." You can't love someone with agape love "at first sight." First sight love is based primarily on physical appearance and charm. Charm is the clever use of social graces—witty conversation, captivating mannerisms, ingratiating actions. Charm reveals nothing about the heart. It doesn't tell you what a person is really like; in fact it often camouflages the true character of the person who employs it. Before you can love with agape love, you must know the other person's heart—the mind, will, and emotions. You can't know anyone that well "at first sight."

Romantic love can also be used of the Devil to deceive you if you're not on guard. I am not prepared, as some preachers and marriage counselors seem to be, to denounce romantic love as having no place in dating or marriage and having no part with agape love. I believe the Bible teaches that there is a place—and an important place—for romantic love in the relationship between a man and woman. Without question, romantic love played a major role in the relationship of Ruth and Boaz, and God assuredly blessed that marriage. Romantic love figured strongly in the marriage of Jacob and Rachel. Otherwise, why did Jacob work seven extra years for Rachel after slaving seven years and being forced to marry her older sister, Leah? Why didn't he just commit himself to love Leah and take her back home with him? Romantic love would not let him turn his back on Rachel. God blessed their relationship and it was one of the vital links in the chain by which he fulfilled his promises to Abraham to make a great nation from his descendants.

What can we say about romantic love, then? Just what should its role be in the male-female relationship? Let me give you my personal opinion. I believe what I am about to say is true, but I am not yet 100 percent certain it's of the Lord.

As I understand it, romantic love is that part of love that springs from the emotions. It's the good feeling that wells up inside you when you see someone who is attractive to you. There's nothing wrong with that feeling. God gave it to you. He meant for you to enjoy it, and he gave it to you for a purpose. It's part of the complex system of attractions he uses to draw you to the one he wants you to choose as your life mate.

But be careful to hear me out on this, because romantic love can be captured by the Devil and used to sweep you off the course God has planned for your life. You've heard the saying, "Love is blind." Well, that saying was coined in reference to romantic love. Remember, I said this type of love springs from the emotions. The emotions have no eyes of their own, but they can cause the mind to see only what they want it to see. And they can cause the will to do only what they want it to do. That's why romantic love, standing alone, is so dangerous. It's guided by the emotions, and the emotions are blind.

Now, if the mind and will are controlled by the Lord and the emotions are guided and controlled by the mind and will, that's a different story. God can take those emotions and use them to make your date life and your marriage happy and beautiful experiences. Romantic love is the frosting on the cake of your relationship. You should feel something special for the person you're going to spend the rest of your life with. God didn't plan marriage to be a drudgery.

God himself loves with his emotions. The Bible is full of texts that show God feels great emotion—greater than we mortals can ever feel—in his love for us.

Jesus said, "These things I have spoken unto you that your joy might be full." What is joy if it isn't an emotion?

I appreciate the warnings that many well-meaning pastors

and counselors have issued against romantic love. But I am
convinced it's wrong to tell young people they shouldn't feel
anything for the person they want to marry. I believe this is
telling them they shouldn't experience any emotional
satisfaction from their relationship. It might be possible to
build a marriage without the emotional aspects of true love,
but show me a marriage like that and I'll show you one that
is missing out on the joy that God intended for marriage to
give men and women.

The shortest verse in the Bible gives evidence of the
emotional aspect of agape love. In John 11:35, as Jesus went
toward the tomb of Lazarus, a man he loved, it's recorded
that "Jesus wept." You don't weep without feeling.
Romantic love is simply emotion, felt between a man and a
woman. Controlled by God, it can add beauty and joy to the
relationship.

One last word on the subject of romantic love· It should be
allowed to develop only late in the dating relationship, after
spiritual oneness has been well established, when physical
maturity and other factors make marriage a realistic option.
Up to that point, allowing romantic love to bloom would be
violating God's order and opening the door to serious
problems.

While agape love includes the emotions, it's not confined
to the emotions. It involves the entire personality—the will
and the mind as well as the emotions. The one true source of
agape love is God himself. The Bible says "love is of God"
and that those who love are born of God and know God (1
John 4:7).

Because God is the source of agape love, the mind and
will of a person who experiences such love are controlled by
God. That person's emotions are also controlled. Feelings
are not allowed to run rampant and dominate the person's
thought process and decisions. The person who loves with
God's kind of love responds with controlled reactions to
everything that happens to him. He is in charge of every
situation—because God is in charge of him.

In the passage known as the "love chapter" of the Bible, 1
Corinthians 13, the Apostle Paul gives a marvelous picture of
a life dominated by agape love· To visualize such a life,

think of some common real-life situations. Imagine the usual, human-nature response to these situations. Then examine the agape-controlled reaction listed by Paul. Beginning with verse 4, your chart could look something like this:

SITUATION—A person does not behave as you desired or expected.
HUMAN REACTION—Impatience, exasperation.
AGAPE REACTION—Patience, kindness.

SITUATION—A person excels, receives acclaim.
HUMAN REACTION—Envy, resentment.
AGAPE REACTION—Rejoicing (Rom. 12:15).

SITUATION—A person reveals desire to develop talent, fulfill visions for life.
HUMAN REACTION—Possessiveness toward other person, attempt to push self forward.
AGAPE REACTION—Yielding to other's desire, offering of encouragement.

SITUATION—Opportunity arises to build yourself up at other's expense.
HUMAN REACTION—Seizing of opportunity, satisfying self-interest.
AGAPE REACTION—Putting welfare, happiness of others first.

SITUATION—Things go wrong, contrary to your wishes.
HUMAN REACTION—Irritation, anger.
AGAPE REACTION—Peace and gentleness.

SITUATION—A person falls into evil behavior pattern.
HUMAN REACTION—Rejoicing, feeling of being superior to the fallen person.
AGAPE REACTION—Weeping, prayer for the fallen one to be restored.

From this chart, which is by no means complete, you can easily see that agape has got to be from God. Human nature does not, and cannot, respond to these life situations with agape love. Human nature is frail and diseased. But God is all-powerful.

Human nature is quick to give up on people. But there's no limit to God's willingness to forgive. Human nature abandons hope when the going gets tough. God's hope never fades. And those are the qualities that radiate from the life of the person possessed with agape—God's forbearance, God's trust, God's hope.

Finally, when the emotional aspect of love gains control in an engagement or marriage, changing situations tend to affect the stability of the relationship. For instance, a husband and wife will be deeply "in love" early in their marriage. But then responsibilities and hardships enter the picture. Neither had counted on problems and pressures arising. They had both thought that after boy meets girl, the two were supposed to "live happily ever after." They didn't know life involved hard work and disappointment and the need to adjust to each other and be used of God to develop each other's character and personality. As a result, when the changes come, the emotional aspect of love is unable to cope. Romantic love weakens and fades.

When that happens, one or the other will come out with what he or she believes to be the tragic truth: "I just don't love you any more." What that pathetic person sees as a loss of love, though, is really just a loss of an emotional high. Romantic love, not supported by a growing and developing God-controlled agape love, simply cannot, as a rule, weather the storms of life.

That brings us to the truly wonderful thing about agape love. It never fades. In 1 Corinthians 13:8 we read: "Love never faileth." Three things endure forever—faith, hope and love And the greatest of these is love—agape love.

HOW LOVE GROWS

Engagement is a serious time. It's a time of planning and sharing goals for the future. It's also a time, however, for continuing a most important activity that should begin in the latter stages of dating—the building of agape love for the dating partner.

The foundation for building agape love for the one whom God has chosen to be your life mate is complete surrender of your heart to God. Since God is the source of agape, you must depend on him to fill you with his kind of love. You need to commit your love to God every day, preferably every morning. Start the day by saying, "Lord, I'm depending on you for love for my life mate, because I know mere human love is weak and unreliable." Then ask God: "How do you want me to express your love today?" You should be doing this with your Bible open. The Bible is all about love. It's a regular "how-to" manual on the subject. If you've been reading the Bible, God has said something to you about love. When you ask how he wants you to express your love, write down his answer, the love principle he has impressed on your heart.

Maybe one day God will say, "Express my love, and yours, with words today." If so, think of the kind of words God uses to express love in his Word. Words of comfort, advice and counsel, compassion. Words of encouragement. Words that convey a willingness on your part to invest whatever it takes of yourself to meet, within the boundaries of God's will, the needs of your life mate.

On other days, God may tell you to express your love with actions. Think about the kind of actions God used in expressing his love. Giving, service, self-sacrifice, assistance. Then be on the alert for the opportunities God will provide for you to express love in some of these ways.

As you build agape love toward your life mate, God will provide you with a sure way to check your progress. You can check how well you're doing by observing your life mate. Your life mate becomes a mirror reflecting back God's love. As you see agape love reflected in the life of your life mate, you will realize that you are seeing the image of God's love growing in you.

Human love isn't destroyed in the process of building agape love. Human love is merely transformed into God's everlasting kind of love, changed and amplified until it becomes some-thing dependable, joyful, and fulfilling.

You don't get "lovesick" with agape love. Agape doesn't make you sick. It makes you well. If you see a couple moping around, sniffling and looking beaten down, you can be sure they haven't developed a mature, agape type of love. The world has the idea that love ought to bring heartache and tears. A popular song of another era said, "This can't be love because I feel too good." That's the world's idea of what love should do to you—it should make you sad. God's idea is that it should make you glad. "That my joy might remain in you, and that your joy might be full," Jesus said (John 15:11).

A man I know had a houseful of daughters, and he was telling me that he could never use his telephone because it always had one of his girls crying on it. You can get hooked on emotions. You can get to the point that you don't feel good unless you're feeling bad. You can come to the point that you enjoy those little emotional upheavals so much that you do things to bring them on. If you go two days without a "lovers' quarrel," a crying jag and a mushy, sobbing "making up" session, you think you're not "in love" any more.

That's not God's kind of love. That's the Devil trying to get you on an emotional trip so he can weaken your relationship with your life mate and thwart God's purpose for your life. If you want to have a happy and fulfilling marriage and a stable home for your family, stay away from the kind of love that makes you sick. Develop the kind that makes you well. Develop God's agape love.

PART TWO

THE RIGHT MATE

INTRODUCTION

Tucked away within the Ten Commandments, and too often
overlooked by casual readers of the Bible, lie a handful of
words that should make all of us stop and think seriously
about every decision of life. Those words are: ". . . I the Lord
thy God am a jealous God, visiting the iniquity of the fathers
upon the children unto the third and fourth generation . . ."
(Ex. 20:5).

Did you ever stop to think that your sins are going to affect
your children, your children's children, and their children,
down to the fourth generation? Suppose you and your mate
had four children, each of them married and had four
children, and so on down through the fourth generation. Do
you realize how many people would be directly affected by
your disregard of God's counsel and instructions? The number
would be 682. And those are only the ones who would be
directly affected. Those whose lives would in turn be touched
and marred by the 682 people would run into the thousands
and tens of thousands.

If you've never thought about this chain reaction effect of
your sinful actions, you should think about it now as it relates
to your choice of a mate and your preparations for marriage.
Disregard for God's guidelines in this crucial decision can have
a stronger impact on your children and grandchildren than
almost any other type of sin.

Engagement is the time for developing oneness of the soul with the person whom you have tentatively chosen to be your life mate. As you enter this more intimate stage of sharing your deepest thoughts and future hopes, you and your mate-to-be will also have opportunity to detect any flaws in your spiritual relationship.

During this stage of your relationship, it may be that the Lord will use your partner to reveal some deficiency in your own spiritual development, some lack that would hinder the two of you from becoming one in soul. Or it may be that you will detect some deficiency in your betrothed. If so, through the wisdom and power of the Holy Spirit, see that the deficiency is overcome during the engagement period. Don't go on into marriage believing that physical oneness will correct the problem. It won't. It may even aggravate it.

The engagement period is your last chance to develop soul oneness with the person you believe is to be your life mate. If you can't do it there, the odds are very much against your ever doing it later, as the adjustments imposed by marriage complicate your interpersonal relationship.

The Word of God contains principles to guide us in forming soul oneness during the engagement period. Essentially, these principles instruct us to build, during this period, the qualities essential to a lasting and fulfilling marriage. The number of qualities that contribute to successful marriage and enrich the relationship is almost infinite. But it's possible to single out some qualities that are absolutely essential—qualities without which a marriage has little chance of success. One well-known Bible scholar and counselor has narrowed the number of these basic qualities to seven. They are:

1. A total personal commitment to Christ.
2. Self-acceptance.
3. Respect for authority.
4. A forgiving spirit.
5. Purity.
6. Awareness of purpose.
7. Financial responsibility.

Now, consider these qualities one at a time. If you're thinking seriously about entering an engagement relationship with someone, or if you're already into that stage, you would do well to examine that person's life carefully with these qualities in mind. How many of these qualities do you find exhibited in his or her life in any degree? Which ones need to be developed from scratch? Which need much further development?

Subject yourself to the same examination. Before you go to the altar to exchange wedding vows, you and your partner should both have substantially overcome any weaknesses in these basic areas.

Let's look at the danger of entering a marriage with any of these qualities lacking in you or your partner. Also, let's consider some ways to proceed in developing each of these qualities during the engagement period.

FIVE
COMMITMENT TO CHRIST

A relationship in which one partner is a non-Christian may seem happy and secure on the surface. If the boy is the non-Christian, his behavior toward the girl may be more courteous and respectful than some of the Christian boys she has known. A girl who isn't committed may appear to be "nicer" than many Christian girls. But sooner or later, trouble almost invariably develops.

The Christian girl, who is aware of the boy's responsibility for spiritual leadership, may try to force the non-Christian boy to lead in this area. Not being spiritual or capable of being guided by the Holy Spirit, the boy will be unable to fulfill the girl's expectations. Sensing the pressure, he may react with annoyance. First, he won't like his partner's exposing what she regards as a weakness in him. He will react defensively. He may also regard her pressure on him to become spiritual as an infringement on his personal rights. "You believe the way you want to believe and I'll believe as I want to believe," he is likely to say. The result will often be a recurring series of arguments. These can lead to deep resentments on the part of both and the beginning of an estrangement.

As she realizes her mate won't fulfill her need for spiritual leadership, the girl may seek that leadership from other sources. She may plunge herself into all sorts of church activities, Bible studies, and prayer groups. She may look for spiritual leadership among her friends or relatives.

This can easily serve to make matters worse in a hurry. The boy—usually at this stage he is the husband—senses the committed girl's lack of confidence in him. He resents her growing reliance on other persons and on activities that do not involve him. More often than not, these resentments prompt him to try to force or lure her away from these outside sources of competition.

As committed as she herself is, the girl may develop guilt feelings as the marriage relationship deteriorates. She may feel God is punishing her for marrying a nonbeliever. In a desperate effort to atone for her "sin," she goes overboard in an attempt to raise her children to be strong Christians.

While bringing up children in the nurture and admonition of the Lord is the responsibility of every parent, it's always a mistake to try to force belief down a child's throat. Children are smart. They know when something is being done from the wrong motives. Sometimes, by the grace of God, children survive such parental misbehavior and grow up to be good Christians. But in many cases they rebel when they are old enough to leave home, or before, and once they get away from God it's almost impossible to get them back.

The mother's overstepping with the kids also evokes a further adverse reaction from the husband. He perceives that the children are being drawn away from him. He may fight back by coddling them, refusing to discipline them properly and spoiling them with gifts and treats. Or he may reject them entirely, refusing to have anything to do with them. "They're your children," he may remind the mother pointedly when she has trouble handling them. His resentment may even become violent at times, the violence being directed at either the mother or the children or both. Feeling that the mother, and perhaps also his own children, "look down on him," he may begin to seek fulfillment of his needs from other sources. When that stage arrives, the marriage is in serious danger; the home is threatened with disintegration.

Equally serious problems often result from a committed boy marrying a nonbelieving girl.

The gravest danger in matches of this kind is that the boy will ultimately drift away from his commitment to the Lord.

Many strong men have fallen to the powerful influences of pagan wives. It happened to Samson. It happened to Solomon.

But defection from the Lord isn't the only danger confronting the man married to an unbelieving wife. Another is that she may not accept the principle that the husband is the head of the household. She may also "try to be boss." Or she may at least insist on "being her own boss." That's not God's plan for marriage, and it almost always produces devastating conflict.

Still another peril is that she may interpret his attempts at spiritual leadership as "preaching" to her. She may perceive it as evidence that he thinks he's "better" than she is. The truth of the saying, "Hell hath no fury like a woman scorned," has been demonstrated countless times through similar situations. The least damaging reaction she is likely to have is one of sullen bitterness and moodiness. Many times her resentment will go beyond that, finding expression in open contentiousness. If the wife feels that her needs are not met in the marriage relationship, she may even begin to search for sources outside the home to meet those needs. The result can be unfaithfulness and dissolution of the marriage.

In this type of marriage, as in the one in which the boy was not committed to Christ, the children stand to suffer. The mother may spoil them to get their affection. She may try to turn them against their "self-righteous" father. Or she may, either literally or in effect, simply abandon them for the pursuit of her own self-gratification.

In the scenarios I have just painted, you may have seen the outline of your own marriage problems, or those of other couples you know. Lack of a basic commitment to Christ, on the part of the husband or wife or both, lies at the bottom of many of today's shattered marriages.

Most of these marriages could be salvaged if both partners were committed Christians. As I pointed out earlier, this commitment should be made by both partners even before dating is begun. Certainly, Christian boys and girls should make sure of the other partner's commitment before entering the engagement phase of their relationship. In cases in which the couple has already married, with one partner lacking a true personal relationship with Christ, there is still hope, however. God, praise his name, can pick up the pieces of any relationship and put them together according to his blueprint if those involved will only let him.

There are a few simple do's and don'ts that should be followed by the Christian partner in his or her relationship with a nonbelieving mate. These are:

Don't argue with the nonbeliever about spiritual things

Don't nag the nonbeliever either to lead or follow in spiritual matters. The Bible tells us nonbelievers can't "receive the things of the Spirit of God, neither can he know them" (1 Cor. 2:14).

Don't adhere to biblical morals in a way that suggests smugness or a "holier than thou" attitude. Of course, the nonbeliever may accuse you of such an attitude, even when you are simply obeying the will of God. But don't be guilty of self-righteousness. The mark of true righteousness is humility.

Don't try to compensate for the nonbelieving partner's lack of spirituality by overdoing religious activities. You can't fulfill another person's spiritual responsibilities.

Don't give in to guilt feelings, which the Devil can use to trick you into conduct that only aggravates the problems.

Do pray, both for guidance in your behavior and for the Holy Spirit to perform his work of conviction and salvation in the heart of the nonbeliever.

Do give a faithful witness. Your life should be a constant testimony to the love and saving grace of the Lord Jesus Christ. And you should present a tactful verbal witness at any time you feel impressed that the Lord is providing you with the opportunity to do so.

Do seek the prayers of other committed Christians for the lost mate.

Do request other Christians to seek the leadership of the Holy Spirit in witnessing to the nonbelieving mate, taking care to avoid pressure or tactlessness that could harden the unbeliever's heart.

Do let it be known that the unbelieving mate is welcome to accompany you to worship services, but avoid any suggestion of pressure or trickery. If the unbeliever refuses to go, show no disappointment or resentment.

Even if both marriage partners have received Jesus Christ as Savior, they can experience problems in their relationship. Often, this is the result of failing to develop spiritual oneness through Christian growth during the dating and engagement stages. Christian couples experiencing such troubles should first examine their devotional lives. Are you reading and studying the Bible daily? Are you meditating on God's Word—that is, thinking about it with a view to applying it to your life? Are you writing it on your heart through memorization so that it is constantly available for the Holy Spirit to "bring to your remembrance" (John 14:26) in every life situation? And finally—this is the tough one—do you realize that as Christians you are ordained to suffer some unpleasantries, because there are some things you simply cannot learn except through tribulation and trial (Phil. 1:29)?

If you had to answer no to any of those questions, then that could well be the problem for you to correct in getting your marriage to conform to God's pattern of love, beauty and oneness.

SIX
SELF-ACCEPTANCE

When asked which is the great commandment in the law of
God, Jesus answered with words familiar to all who are
acquainted with the Scriptures. "Thou shalt love the Lord
thy God with all thy heart, and with all thy soul, and with all
thy mind," he answered. Then he went right on to pinpoint
the second greatest commandment: "Thou shalt love thy
neighbor as thyself" (Matt. 22:37-39).

While most people know this passage, most overlook what
I have come to regard as its key words. Those words appear
in the little prepositional phrase found at the end—"as
thyself."

It's impossible for anyone to love another, even God,
unless he loves himself. I heartily disagree with much that
modern psychology tells us, but with that idea I find myself
in complete accord. God desires us to love him. He wants us
to love our neighbor. But Jesus' words indicate that he is
well aware that we must love ourselves. I am convinced that
much of his message to us is intended to convince us that we
should love ourselves, that we can love ourselves, and that
God has gone to great lengths to make us aware of some
very good reasons why we should love ourselves.

If nothing else can convince you that you should love
yourself, the very fact that God made you should be enough
to do so. Look at the loving passage from Psalm 139
(NASB), where God reveals the wonderful fact that he is, in
reality, your Creator:

"For thou didst form my inward parts;
Thou didst weave me in my mother's womb.
I will give thanks to Thee, for I am fearfully and
    wonderfully made;
Wonderful are Thy works, and my soul knows it very well.
My frame was not hidden from Thee,
When I was made in secret, and skillfully wrought in the
    depths of the earth.
Thine eyes have seen my unformed substance;
    And in Thy book they were all written,
The days that were ordained for me,
    When as yet there was not one of them." (verses 13-16).

Yes, God made you, and he made you the way you are for
a purpose. His ultimate purpose for making you the way
you are is that your life might give glory to his name.

But God didn't just make you and then forget you. His
interest in you continues forever, its intensity never
diminishing. He reveals that truth in the very next words of
Psalm 139:

"How precious also are Thy thoughts to [toward] me, O
    God!
How vast is the sum of them!
If I should count them, they would outnumber the sand.
    When I awake, I am still with Thee." (verses 17-18).

If God made you, and his thoughts about you—little and
insignificant and unworthy as you may seem to yourself—are
without limit, then certainly you have reason to consider
yourself of some importance in his scheme of things. And if
you are important to God, then you have every justification for
holding yourself in high esteem—not pridefully, but gratefully.
You can humbly say to yourself, "I'm important, because God
made me and has a plan for my life—a plan that only I can
fulfill." You can say with gratitude, "I love myself because
God has made me worthy of love, having washed and cleansed

me with the blood of his Son." You can say, "I can accept myself because God accepts me, in Christ; I respect myself because God respects me and has high expectations for me."

Do you really want to know how highly God prizes you? Then look at Paul's inspired words to the Christians at Ephesus. In Ephesians 1:18 (NASB) he says: "I pray that the eyes of your heart may be enlightened, so that you may know what is the hope of His calling, what are the riches of the glory of His inheritance in the saints."

Think about those last words for a moment. "His inheritance in the saints." What is the antecedent of that pronoun "his"? It's God. Paul is talking about God's inheritance. And where is that inheritance found? In the saints! And who are the saints? Those who believe, those who have received Christ as Savior and Lord.

Now put it all together. God considers himself rich— exceedingly wealthy—because of the inheritance he has in those who believe in him. That means all Christians. That means me. It means you. *You* are God's inheritance. That's how important you are to him. You're what he is living for, what he is looking forward to. You are his everything.

You *can* love yourself, knowing how much God loves you!

Then, of course, the irrefutable proof that God loves you and considers you worthy of self-acceptance and self-love lies in the fact that he gave his only begotten Son in order to have fellowship with you. "But God demonstrates His own love toward you, in that while you were yet a sinner Christ died for you." That's Romans 5:8 (NASB). I just changed the pronouns from "us" to "you," to emphasize that in this great verse the Holy Spirit is talking about you, and about God's irrepressible love for you.

Yes, God knew before he created you that you couldn't fulfill his commandment to love your neighbor unless you first loved yourself. That's why he has gone to such lengths in his Word to convince you that you have every right to love and accept yourself.

And, of course, it stands to reason that if you must love yourself before you can love your neighbor as you should, you must certainly love yourself before you can love your mate as you should. You can close the gate, lock the doors, draw the drapes, and shut your neighbor out—at least for a few

refreshing moments. But you can't shut out your mate. You're
bound to this other person in everything you do—really, in
every thought you think. You're committed to share with your
mate every annoyance, frustration, or trial, every triumph, joy,
or success that life brings to either of you. If you don't accept
yourself, you can't relate to another person in a spirit of oneness
in this most intimate of all relationships. You can't hope to
cope with the stresses such a close association with another
individual inevitably produces.

If one or the other of the partners in a marriage lacks self-
acceptance, an almost unlimited assortment of problems can
develop. Let me give you just two hypothetical examples,
constructed from the real-life experience of marriages in which
self-acceptance was an insidious problem.

Molly marries Fred, who has never quite been able to accept
himself. Because of his inferiority complex, he plunges into all
sorts of activities in an effort to win approval of others. He
throws himself into his job, church work, sports—all with
fanatical zeal. None of these things is bad in itself, but soon
they're taking up all his time. He's seldom around the house,
except to eat and sleep. Molly resents Fred's activities. She feels
that they've stolen his affections from her.

That touches off a second layer of problems. Her rejection of
his activities really puts the skids under Fred's emotions. He
can't understand this woman. Before they were married, she
always seemed thrilled over everything he did. He's disappointed by her attitude, and he lets her know about it. "What
gives?" he asks. "You're not the gal I married any more." That
seems to straighten her out, but only on the surface. She can't
help resenting Fred's time-consuming activities. But to keep
peace in the family, she pretends to be interested in the things
he's doing.

This only adds another spoonful of nitroglycerin to the
brewing nuptial explosion. Still preoccupied with his efforts to
gain approval, he fails to notice the special effort his wife is
making to please him. Self-centered and thoughtless, he even
criticizes her for some of the extra things she tries to do for
him. She reacts by feeling that he never really loved her, that
he married her only to use her.

Then Molly makes a portentious discovery. She finds that
when she has a special need. Fred pays attention to her. When

she's sick with a cold, he brings her aspirin and nosedrops. If she becomes deeply depressed, he puts his arm around her and asks, "What's the matter, honey?" Problems with the children evoke similar responses from the otherwise busy Fred. He really woke up the time she told him Junior had skipped school and gone to an amusement park with a group of pot-smoking boys. She begins to invent little illnesses and problems and to work herself into deep depression just to get his attention.

Fred tries to cheer her up and spend some time helping her with problems. He brings flowers, takes her out to dinner, spends time he could be devoting to his approval-winning activities listening to Molly's woes. But soon he begins to notice that no matter how much he does, it's never enough. If he tries to break away for just one little fishing trip, she goes into a fit of depression or comes up with another big problem to drop on him. Fred's frustration builds to a boiling point. To get away from it all, he throws his tackle box in the station wagon and goes fishing anyway.

After this happens a few times, Molly resorts to other devices to get Fred's attention. She discovers she can make him notice her by doing "little" things that hurt him. She starts flirting with other men, behaving rudely toward his parents, belittling his friends. She fakes illness when he tries to get her to respond to him physically in order to deprive him of sexual gratification. At the least provocation, she flares up in anger toward him.

Soon, finding his physical and emotional needs not being met by his wife, Fred senses a strong temptation to get emotionally and physically involved with other women. At this point the marriage of Fred and Molly is in deep trouble. Whether or not Fred yields to his temptations—some "Freds" do and some don't—it will take a dramatic work of the Lord in both their lives to mend the rift between them and heal the wounds already inflicted. All because one of the marriage partners never learned to accept himself.

Failure of a marriage partner to accept himself often results in undeserved misery for the children, too. It's not uncommon for a father or mother to try to improve his or her self-image by pushing the children into activities the parent wanted to excel in. That's the case with another hypothetical couple, Henry and Harriet. This time it's Harriet who has the self-acceptance hang-up. The children—don't underestimate their perception—quickly recognize that their mother is psychologically dependent on their achievement. The pressures of knowing this creates in them a fear of failure. This leads to insecurity.

Betty, the oldest child, had Harriet's attention all to herself until she was three. That gave her a head start and, with her mother's pushing, she became a bright and precocious little girl. Because Betty demanded all of Harriet's attention, her brother Bobby didn't have an equally stimulating babyhood; Harriet hadn't desired to excel in things boys do, so she didn't push him. Bobby never did the outstanding, mom-pleasing things Betty did. As a result, Harriet "naturally" showed favoritism toward Betty. Bobby felt rejected. He became resentful and aggressive toward Betty. He resented his mother. At home, he became unmanageably rebellious. When he went to school, he quickly fell behind his grade level in academic achievement. School officials recommended clinical testing to determine the problem. The diagnosis: emotionally disturbed. Bobby may be crippled for life.

Self-rejection works some of its greatest evil in the area of family finances. Almost invariably, the self-rejecting partner spends recklessly on items designed to bolster the sagging self-image. This wrecks the budget for food, clothing, and other necessities. If the husband is the self-rejecting partner, he may ask his wife to go to work "temporarily" to help pay the bills. In so doing, he surrenders to his wife part of the provider role which is his responsibility as head of the home. Collecting a paycheck of her own gives the wife a sense of greater rights in deciding how the family income is spent. The husband interprets her insistence on having her say in family budget matters as distrust of his judgment. That aggravates his self-acceptance problem. Feeling a greater need than ever to prove himself, he spends even more recklessly. She becomes more adamant in her demands for a role in financial decision making. The cycle repeats itself. By now, quarreling over money problems dominates their relationship.

Sometimes this running battle over money leads to divorce.

It has been known to lead even to murder or suicide. It always leads to misery. But it almost always pays to look deeper for the source of the trouble. Many times the real problem isn't money at all. Many times it's self-rejection, the simple inability of one marriage partner to accept the person that God created him or her to be.

SIGNS OF THE PROBLEM

Self-rejection betrays itself in a person by several telltale signs. Some attitudes that signal this problem are:

Overemphasis on Clothes. People with a low self-image may try to cover up the problem by becoming flashy, expensive dressers. Or they may go the opposite route and try to get attention by seeing how sloppy and disheveled they can look. There's nothing wrong with dressing neatly, fashionably, and with modesty. But over-attention to clothing is never of the Lord. Jesus said, " . . . be not anxious for your life . . . as to what you shall put on. . . ." (Matt. 6:25, NASB).

Weakness of Faith. Since God drew the design, one who dislikes the design can hardly be expected to love and trust the Designer. The Bible says, "We are His workmanship. . ." (Eph. 2:10, NASB). If we don't really accept the product, we can't have a strong relationship with the Producer.

Inability to Love Others. If we can't love ourselves, we can't love our neighbors—or our wives or husbands or anyone else.

Self-Castigation. A person with a poor self-concept sometimes goes to extremes in one direction or another. Some overcompensate for their inferior feelings and immerse themselves into the comforting waters of self-adulation, or narcissism. More often, though, self-rejection leads to the other extreme—scathing self-criticism. It may take the form of bitter complaints about unalterable physical traits, innate abilities, social heritage, or even parentage. A person who is forever running himself down in the presence of others may try to coat his expressions with layers of false modesty, but the problem is probably a deep sense of self-rejection.

Unfavorable Comparison with Others. Unable to accept himself, the person with a low self-image may habitually compare himself unfavorably with those who possess talents or abilities he lacks. His desire to be different locks him into a hopeless trap of inferiority feelings, since he forever singles out the strongest attributes of others to stack up against his own weakest attributes.

Extreme Shyness. Seeing himself as inferior, this person naturally suspects that others regard him in the same light. As a result, he may avoid exposure to the supposedly critical examination of others by simply avoiding contact with others as much as posssible. He may openly "dislike people" or simply refuse to mix with them.

General Bitterness. One who is down on himself often betrays his inner feelings by being "down on the world." He may be especially cynical toward "the church," "religion" and "do-gooders"—by which he usually means committed Christians. His ultimate bitterness, though, is toward God, whether or not he admits the fact openly.

Perfectionism. The self-rejector may strive tirelessly to gain approval for himself by being perfect in everything he does. He finds it far more devastating to have to admit he is wrong, even about the most insignificant things, than self-accepting persons do. In this attitude, he is in open rebellion against God. God's purpose for man is to glorify God, not himself. "Whether therefore ye eat, or drink, or whatsoever ye do, do all to the glory of God" (1 Cor. 10:31).

When marriages start falling apart, people should look for these signs of self-rejection. If they are found in either partner, lack of self-acceptance may be the root of the marital problem.

After self-rejction has been identified as the problem, there's hope for a solution. Self-acceptance can be built through commitment to a step-by-step spiritual rehabilitation program.

STEPS TO A SOLUTION

1. New Perspective. The first step is to adopt a new perspective. If you've been unable to accept yourself as you are, remember again that God predesigned you before you were born, and that he did so with a purpose in mind. Also remember that God isn't through making you yet. If you've given your life to him by faith in Jesus Christ, you are his workmanship, according to Ephesians 2:10, and that's a continuing action verb. It means God is continuing to mold and shape you into what he wants you to be.

Since God made everyone by a different pattern, avoid comparing yourself to other people. God gave others some things he didn't give you. But he also gave you a lot that he didn't give to others.

Don't give much importance to physical attractiveness. It's just that—attractiveness. It attracts, but that doesn't mean it can necessarily do anything else. Often, the character housed in that attractive person fails to fulfill the promise implied. God's ideal pertains to the inward person. His purpose calls for you to be "conformed to the image of his Son" (Rom. 8:29). He wants your life to be adorned with the "fruit of the spirit . . . love, joy, peace, patience, kindness, goodness, faithfulness, gentleness and self-control" (Gal. 5:22, 23, NASB). If you receive these attributes, through fellowship with Christ, you need never worry about your physical appearance.

2. Redefine Achievement. You need a new definition for achievement, too. In God's eyes, you begin to achieve when you gain the ability to experience his inward ideal for your life. Other successes flow from that. ". . . these things shall be added unto you" (Matt. 6:33). God has a unique message to proclaim through you. If your life is proclaiming that message, you're a brilliant success no matter what your material circumstances may be.

3. Pray for Change. You may have some characteristic that seems an obvious flaw or defect. If so, pray for God to change it if possible—if he so wills—then trust him to answer your prayer according to his faithfulness. If it's his will to change the bothersome trait, he'll do so in his own way and in his own time.

4. Glory in Weakness. Some flaws or defects—as we would define them from the human perspective—may not be that at all. They may be characteristics that God has built into your life for his own purposes. It may not be his will to change those traits. If this becomes apparent to you, then glory in the "defect." Paul said, "I . . . glory . . . in mine infirmities" (2 Cor. 12:5). God can use such attributes for many purposes—to motivate you to develop the inward qualities he desires in you, to enable you to find happiness by serving others rather than being served (as many "attractive" people are), or simply to keep you reminded that you're his.

5. Live by Faith. The fifth step in building self-acceptance is simply to get on with living a life of faith in God. Thank him for the way he has made you thus far. If you find that hard to do, list what you consider your defects and, reviewing the preceding paragraph, think of ways God might want to use these qualities to fulfill his purpose through your life. Commit yourself to be used of God to deliver the unique message he wants to proclaim through your life and to helping reproduce Christlike character in the lives of others.

SEVEN
RESPECT FOR AUTHORITY

This is the age of "do your own thing." The emphasis
everywhere in society is on the rights of the individual, on self-
fulfillment. The rebel is the folk hero of the times. Authority,
usually labeled "the Establishment," is the villain. "The
Establishment," as scornfully defined by the rebel, includes all
forms of authority. It takes in government at every level,
corporate chains of command, cultural traditions, the mores of
society, discipline in the classroom and, perhaps above all,
the child-rearing responsibility of parents in the home. The
rhetoric of the modern rebel defines any assertion of authority
on the part of "the Establishment" as repression, an attempt to
deny the individual his right to choose his own route to
personal fulfillment.

But that line of rhetoric is not of God. It's of the Devil. God
ordained authority in every area of society. He set up systems
of leadership and control in every aspect of human life, from
the state level down to the individual. Without authority, and
respect for it, people could not live and function in community
with one another. Order would evaporate. Society would fly
apart like a clock with a broken mainspring.

Recognition and respect for authority is no more important
in any area of life than in the marriage relationship. If either
marriage partner fails to respect authority and live in
cooperation with it, the marriage faces almost insurmountable
problems.

You must realize, too, that I'm not talking about a resentful acknowledgement of authority and a grudging submission to it. When I say "respect for authority," I mean a heartfelt appreciation for it, a spiritual desire to be in accord with it.

That kind of respect for authority flows from a recognition of the fact that authority is of God and that God ordained it for our benefit. That kind of respect is a commitment to obey authority as the will of God for our lives.

You could take many of today's broken marriages and shattered homes and trace from the wreckage a bitter trail of rebellion against authority.

It usually starts in the home, where children first encounter authority. The boy or girl begins to resist the parents' authority. The parents, detecting what they interpret as stubbornness in the child, become more firm and assertive. This leads to unpleasant clashes of will between child and parent. If parents fail to handle these skirmishes properly, the rebelliousness develops along one of two lines. Either the child becomes increasingly defiant, openly refusing to yield to the parents' will, or else he or she will learn to conform outwardly while continuing to rebel inwardly.

When rebellion is outwardly displayed, it can produce a lot of unpleasantness in the home. But at least it offers some possibility of corrective measures, since it is out in the open and recognized.

Inward rebellion is more dangerous, because it may lurk undetected until habit patterns are so entrenched that they are almost impossible to change. Inward rebellion is the kind that appears again in later life and causes the most trouble in marriages.

Parents, deceived by the outward appearance of conformity, often give undeserved freedom to the child. These grants of liberty are sometimes bribes meant to appease the child after an occasional display of resistance.

The child encounters other sources of authority outside the home, however, and his or her defiance results in clashes with teachers, employers, and perhaps even the police. Because the child appears to be conforming at home, parents sometimes are convinced that their unruly offspring is the victim of unfairness on the part of the authority figures. And sometimes, too, parental pride is involved. The parents will take the part of the child in brushes with authority outside the home because they feel that an admission that the child is at fault will reflect on them and their childrearing ability.

That type of parental self-serving inevitably reinforces the child's rebellious streak. He becomes firm in the cynical belief that society is unfair, that all authority figures are out to prevent him from "doing his thing" as an individual.

Young people in this frame of mind are ripe for the wrong kind of marriage. They're vulnerable to the phony solicitousness of those who say they "understand" them. On the other hand, some of them are skilled at playing the martyr and taking advantage of a truly sympathetic partner.

Parents of the rebellious child often contribute to unsound marriages. They get the mistaken idea that their rebellious young person will be all right once he or she "marries and settles down." With that false hope in mind, they actually pressure the young person to marry without the necessary preparation or maturity.

Young men, beware of the rebellious girl. If she has defied her parents' authority, the school's authority, and society's authority while growing up, she will defy your authority as a husband. She won't accept her role of submission to you as the God-appointed head of the household. She'll resent the confinement of household duties and bearing and rearing children. Unless she is transformed by an act of submission to Jesus Christ, she'll become more of a rebel than ever in the marriage relationship.

And young woman, beware of the rebellious young man. You may expect him to change because you love him and "feel sorry for him." That won't change him. He'll misunderstand your efforts to point out his problems and encourage him to improve. He'll feel that you don't accept him, and he'll resent the pressure you're putting on him. He'll begin to see you as another despised authority figure. "You're just like my mother," he'll fume.

The arrival of children only makes matters worse. The rebellious marriage partner usually takes out his or her frustration on the children. As a result of their own upbringing, rebellious persons often make one of two mistakes in childrearing. They will either be too strict, wishing that their own parents had been stricter with them, or they will be too lenient, feeling that their parents were too strict.

Rebellious partners often let their resentment build to the point that they flatly reject their mates. When this happens, they usually try to force their mates to seek a divorce. They've learned, through a life of resisting authority, to always try to shift blame to someone else. This trait carries over into the marriage relationship.

SIGNS OF THE PROBLEM

You can spot evidences of authority problems in the personality of the boy or girl whom you are dating. When you detect such traits, you should break off the dating relationship. You should not resume dating the rebellious person until his or her life shows unmistakable signs that the problem has been overcome. Usually, those signs won't appear until the person's rebellious spirit has been broken by a faith encounter with the Lord.

The number one characteristic is self-centeredness. If you see a boy or girl building his or her life around personal interests and doing what he or she pleases rather than seeking God's purpose, you can be sure that personality harbors a rebellious spirit.

The rebellious personality also will be characterized by:

—Greed: an insatiable desire for material things.

—Boastfulness: a penchant for pointing to achievements and for exaggerating the importance of accomplishments.

—Pride: a conceited, arrogant demeanor that may be a device to convince others that the rebellious person is pleased with the results of running his or her own life.

—Contempt: a tendency to hold others and their accomplishments in low esteem, a habit of putting together elaborate arguments to discredit the positions taken by authority figures, including God and the Bible.

—Disobedience: a defiance of all rules and guidelines but especially those set forth by parents in the home.

—Ungratefulness: the attitude that "the world owes me a living," a tendency to focus not on what has been received but on what still hasn't been received.

—Profanity: habits of speech and conduct that make continuous display of a disregard for God and spiritual things.

—Insensitivity: Because he or she is wrapped up in his or her own problems and desires, the rebellious person can't love others or care about what happens to them.

God gives people a natural affection for others, especially members of their own families and those closest to them. Those who reject authority lack this natural affection.

—Contentiousness: an inclination to disagree or quarrel with others; an inability to act harmoniously with others.

—Slander: To divert attention from his own shortcomings, the rebellious person finds fault in others, especially persons in authority, and makes distorted and often false statements to discredit them.

—Incontinence: The rebellious person lacks self-control, the ability to refrain from acting on every impulse.

—Viciousness: a fiendish pleasure in making fierce attacks on anyone who "stands in my way," especially authority figures.

—Treachery: an inclination to betray the trust of others, especially authority figures whom the rebellious person sees as interfering in his or her life.

—Recklessness: the trait of being impulsive or rash—a deceptive characteristic since others may interpret it as spunk or daring.

—Conceit: exaggerated self-esteem, especially in comparison with others.

—Sensuality: an almost total focus on pleasure, on gratification of sensual appetites.

—Hypocrisy: While the rebellious person often attacks the "hypocrites" in the church, he or she is often the biggest hypocrite of all. He or she may put on a religious front, pretending to be right with God (while claiming to do so "without going to church"). But he or she denies the power of true Christianity, the supernatural power of Christ indwelling the human life.

In the family, God has ordained the husband to be the principal authority figure, as we have already discussed. So the wife determines whether or not there is a harmonious spirit in the home by whether she submits to her husband's authority or rejects it. But the husband also must submit to authority—to God's authority, first, and to the authorities God has ordained in the world. These include the various arms of government, authority figures on the job, and elsewhere in society.

STEPS TO A SOLUTION

If either partner in the dating situation is rebelling against authority, that problem should be met head-on and conquered before the relationship progresses any further. The problem of rejecting authority can be overcome through faith in the wisdom and power of God.

1. Commitment to Christ. The first step in overcoming resistance to authority, of course, is to make a genuine commitment to Christ. Recognize that God is over all, yield control of your life to him, and acknowledge that he knew what he was doing when he set up systems of authority in this world.

Once you have made this commitment, you can begin to discover in the Word of God certain precepts about authority. When you come to understand these precepts, you will begin to see authority from God's perspective. Then you will appreciate what God is attempting to do in your life by placing you under various authority figures and, instead of resenting authority, you will welcome it and look forward to the benefits you can gain by cooperation. Let's consider some of the most important Biblical precepts concerning authority.

First, realize that God regards you as a jewel that needs to be shaped and polished—a "diamond in the rough." In Malachi 3:17, the Lord says, " . . . they shall be mine. . . in that day when I make up my jewels . . ." When you accept Christ as your Savior, you don't enter into the Kingdom of God already perfect. You enter as raw material that God can work with to make what he wants of you. Submit to him and let him finish the work he wants to do in you and through you.

Second, realize that the authority figures God puts over you are his instruments for molding and shaping your life into the image he wants it to bear. Romans 13:1 commands us to submit to authority, because "the powers that be are ordained of God." And in Romans 8:28 God informs us through Paul that all things—including the unpleasant encounters we have with authority—work together for good to them that love God and are called for his purpose. God uses the pressures of authority to do a work in our lives. You need never fear that the forces of authority will warp your life, because they're in the hands of God and under his control. God knows how to use his instruments, even when they don't know they're being used, and his gentle sculpting hand won't slip.

2. *Yield to God's Instruments.* With the loving purpose of God in mind, you should be able to think positively about authority. You should be able to think only of how God uses it to bring forth your true potential as a member of God's family. You should gladly yield to God's instruments.

But there is a negative side to the issue, and you need to be aware of it. God has issued some clear warnings as to what happens to those who refuse to submit to authority.

If you reject one of God's authority instruments, he will only raise up another—one more firm and demanding than the one you rejected. Proverbs 17:11 states that those who seek only rebellion will have "a cruel messenger" sent against them.

Continual rebellion brings even harsher measures. God won't put up with something he can't use. He keeps pounding on it. If it refuses to be used in the form it's in, he will shatter it and try to work with the pieces. "He, that being often reproved hardeneth his neck," God says, "shall suddenly be destroyed, and that without remedy" (Proverbs 29:1).

If the authority figures you resist are nonbelievers, you may find yourself held accountable by God for their souls. Often, when an authority figure is rejected by a Christian, he in turn rejects the rebellious Christian. But he doesn't stop there. He also rejects the God whom the rebellious Christian professes to serve.

Some of the hardest people to win to Christ are those who

have had disagreeable conflicts with mule-headed, authority-rejecting Christians. God holds Christians accountable for those who are turned away from Christ by their rebellious behavior (1 Cor. 3:11-15).

To sum up the points made so far, problems with authority stem from two basic sources:

1. Improper attitude toward authority.
2. A desire for independence.

You can correct your attitude toward authority by realizing authority is of God and that you have been placed under certain authority figures so that God can use them to do a work in your life. Then you can understand that independence, in the sense of your doing your own thing and not being accountable to God or to others for how you live your life, is simply not a part of God's program. He has a purpose for your life.

3. Earn Your Independence. Your only proper response to a loving God who wants the best for you is to let him show you his purpose for you and prepare you to fulfill it. God does want you to have a certain independence from authority figures other than himself, but you don't get that kind of independence handed to you as a gift. You earn it.

You earn independence, not by defying and resisting authority, but by submitting to authority. Do what your authority figures tell you to do, what they expect you to do. Learn to enjoy obeying their instructions and pleasing them with your performance. Practice figuring out the reasons behind the things authorities demand of you. If you try to understand, you may be surprised how often you will agree that what they want you to do is actually the very thing you should do.

4. Explore Alternatives. Even if you do all of these things, you still may find that you have some conflicts with authority. When clashes occur, try discussing the problem reasonably with the person in charge. Be prepared to suggest an alternate approach to the task at hand. You may get permission to get the job done in a way that will be more pleasant to you and just as pleasing to the authority.

Learning to cooperate with authority requires a constant

walk of faith. But it's a necessary accomplishment for any young man or young woman who wants to have a lasting, fulfilling marriage.

If either you or your potential mate resents authority, get that problem under control before you get married. If you're already married, get to work on the problem through the wisdom and power of God right now. You can't have a healthy marriage until you understand God's principles concerning authority and start living in compliance with those principles.

EIGHT
A FORGIVING SPIRIT

Another quality that is absolutely essential to genuine oneness in marriage is a true sense of forgiveness. I like to call it a Spirit of forgiveness. I use the capital "S" advisedly, because I don't believe anybody can understand the all-forgiving nature of God except through the illumination of the Holy Spirit.

God makes it abundantly clear in his Word that everyone has sinned (Rom. 3:23). He makes it equally clear that the only remedy for our sinful condition is to accept the atonement God provides through the blood of Christ (1 John 2:2). When a sinner accepts Jesus Christ as Savior and Lord, the Bible says he enters into eternal fellowship with the Father, the Son, and other believers and that "the blood of Jesus Christ . . . [continually] cleanseth us from all sin" (1 John 1:7).

That's a tremendous spiritual truth. It's a basic principle of the Christian life. If you don't understand it, you will have guilt problems. The Devil can use guilt to destroy your Christian witness, to rob you of the joy of your salvation, to ruin your marriage, and wreck your home.

Do you know how the Devil blinds you to this great truth about God's forgiveness? By giving you a limited concept of God. Satan tries to keep you from believing that God is as good and merciful as he really is. He gets you to think,

"Well, God has forgiven me for some things but he hasn't forgiven me for *that* sin."

But that's a lie. God says the blood of Jesus Christ, his Son, has cleansed you of *all* your past sins and is continually cleansing you day by day and moment by moment of the sins you are now committing.

Your part is merely to acknowledge those sins, set your heart against repeating them (that's called repentance) and take God's word that he has forgiven you as he promises he will.

There is another dimension to the Spirit of forgiveness that you need to be aware of as you consider marriage, or as you look for spiritual insights to strengthen your marriage. You are not only to recognize and accept the fact that all your sins—every last one of them—has been forgiven if you've accepted Christ as your Savior. You are also to be aware that God expects you to have toward others the same forgiving attitude that he has toward you. "For if ye forgive men their trespasses, your heavenly Father will also forgive you: But if ye forgive not men their trespasses, neither will your Father forgive your trespasses" (Matt. 6:14, 15).

If your spirit of forgiveness falls short, either with respect to God's forgiveness of you or your forgiveness of others, it affects all of your relationships. It can cause serious problems in marriage. Let's consider briefly how a faulty sense of forgiveness works to create marital problems.

PROBLEM: GUILTY CONSCIENCE

If the problem is failure to realize that past sins have been cleansed, the specific source of trouble will be a guilty conscience. If you feel guilty about things you've done in the past, you'll crave the comfort of close relationships. Yet you'll tend to keep people at a distance from you. You won't want anyone to get too close to you, because you'll fear they may discover your secret sin and reject you or expose you.

Your guilt feelings, then, will stand in the way of your developing oneness with your mate. Your mate or potential mate will naturally want to know about your past and will try to get you to talk about it. But you won't want to talk about it. You'll avoid the issue; you'll try to change the subject. Soon your date or your mate will get the message: There are certain areas of your life that are closed to others—especially to your partner.

You may try to get rid of your guilt feelings by getting involved in religious activities or civic projects, but you won't find peace in these things. The Bible warns that "he who conceals his transgressions will not prosper," that only those who confess and forsake them will find compassion (Prov. 28:13, NASB). Getting busy or getting "churchy" won't help you with your guilt problem.

Your guilt will interfere with your ability to focus your attention on your mate. He or she will sense that you are not listening during conversations. You won't be able to look your mate in the eye. Your mate will interpret these traits as lack of interest in him or her. The feeling of being neglected will prompt your mate to do things—perhaps annoying things—to get your attention.

Your mate soon will begin to assume the blame for your inattention. He or she will try to justify your conduct as dedication to all the good causes you are involved in, but a bitterness begins to build up inwardly not just toward you but toward your activities as well.

At the same time, you become disillusioned with people. No matter how much you do for them, they never seem to appreciate you. You try hard to help others, but you're disappointed in their response. You become an expert in defending yourself and criticizing others. You get to be a master at running others down and building yourself up. You need that, you see, because your guilty conscience won't stay quiet. It keeps telling you what you really are. You're engaged in a shouting match with that aching conscience, pointing to your good deeds and good works and screaming, "I'm not like you say I am; I'm good; look at all the good I'm doing," while your conscience stabs an accusing finger in your chest and yells, "Whom are you kidding—look at the bad you've done."

Your mate catches the brunt of your critical spirit and your defensiveness and reacts in a way that causes you to resent him or her.

This problem can grow until you're disillusioned with almost everyone. You're probably disillusioned most of all

with Christians whom you perceive as being better than you.
You want their attention and approval, but because of your
own aloofness you haven't been able to form the close relationships that would win you that degree of acceptance.
Your disappointment with Christians gives you an excuse to
backslide. You go back to your old attitudes and behavior
patterns, the very ones that gave you the guilt feelings in the
first place.

In that backslidden condition, you're no match for the
problems that have developed in your relationship with your
mate or potential mate. If you're married, you're ripe for a
divorce unless you experience the kind of change that only a
touch from the Holy Spirit can give you. If you're not
married yet, you shouldn't get married until you have been
freed from your guilt. In your present state, a marriage
would bring nothing but conflict and misery.

Barbara (that's not her real name) was a Christian girl
who married a boy with a guilty conscience. Though active
in her church she was, like many young people, not firmly
grounded in the Word of God. Her husband was active, too,
but for a different reason. He didn't love God; he simply
hoped to quiet his guilty conscience by doing good works.

When Barbara's husband became disillusioned with
church people, he started delving into books and articles that
detracted from Christianity, that questioned the Bible and
pointed out so-called inconsistencies and contradictions in
the Scriptures. At first, Barbara tried to defend her beliefs.
But soon, like Eve in the Garden of Eden, she let a seed of
doubt be planted. Her doubts and frustrations soon caused
her to drift away from church attendance and Bible study
and prayer. She, too, began to avoid the fellowship of other
Christians.

As Barbara began to think more like her hypercritical
husband, their relationship deteriorated more rapidly than
ever. Seeing Barbara backslide only aggravated her husband's
bitterness and disillusionment.

Then, through a series of events brought about by God in
answer to the prayers of some concerned Christian friends,
the husband came under conviction by the Holy Spirit and
made a clean confession of all his sins. God's forgiveness
restored to him the joy of his salvation, as the Bible

promises. He went home overflowing with the good news.
He thought Barbara would rejoice with him as soon as she
knew what had happened.

But Barbara's fellowship with the Lord had been severely
damaged. It took months of prayer and her husband's loving
example before she yielded to the wooing of the Spirit and
returned to her walk with the Lord.

Your guilty conscience, you see, affects more than just
your own life. It affects the relationship others have with
Christ. After months of misery and strife, Barbara got rid of
her confusion and had her relationship with Jesus renewed.
Some who have been so disillusioned have never been
restored.

"But whoso shall offend one of these little ones which
believe in me, it were better for him that a millstone were
hanged about his neck, and that he were drowned in the
depth of the sea," Jesus said (Matt. 18:6).

If you have a guilty conscience, you would do well to let
God rid you of it right now. If you hesitate, you could some
day face a terrible judgment because of what your attitudes
and actions have done to others.

SIGNS OF THE PROBLEM

A guilty conscience betrays itself through certain attitudes
and behavior patterns. If you are dating a person and
considering engagement, you should pause if you spot any
of these signs in your prospective mate's personality. If you
are already married and having problems, these signs could
give you a clue to the basic cause of the trouble.

A guilty conscience impedes effective Christian witnessing.
If your date or mate seems to be a dedicated Christian,
tireless church worker, etc., but can't witness effectively, it
may indicate a guilty conscience.

Notice, I didn't say that a person with a guilty conscience
can't witness at all, only that such a person normally can't
witness effectively. Usually, a guilty conscience will do one
of two things to a Christian. It will either lock his lips with
fear or false timidity, or else it will loosen his tongue at both
ends, giving him an offensive and insensitive boldness.
Either way, his witness becomes ineffective.

A guilty conscience will also sometimes move a person to do good in a bad way. Have you ever known anyone like that? He seems to be trying to do all sorts of good, but he is always hurting more than he is helping. He tramples people underfoot in his rush to get good works done. That's often a sign of a guilty conscience. A bad conscience drives him to do good in order to get attention and approval, but in the process he abandons God's priorities. He forgets that the primary purpose in life is to be a servant to others. In his determination to build himself up to overcome a guilty conscience, he injures others rather than serving them.

Nervousness and poor eye contact are other characteristics that sometimes indicate a guilty conscience.

A person with a guilty conscience also will often be on the defensive. Because his guilt feelings condemn him day and night, he feels compelled to destroy anything that would make him look bad in the eyes of others. He strives to justify or excuse everything he does.

Fears, usually irrational fears, characterize a person with a guilty conscience. The basic fear is the fear of being found out. That leads to fear of punishment, and that in turn results in the fear of terrible things happening. Proverbs 28:1 describes the problem succinctly: "The wicked flee when no man pursueth."

A tendency to be accident-prone can be a sign of a guilty conscience. Actually, the "accidents" are not accidental. Thinking himself deserving of punishment, the person with the guilty conscience allows himself to be injured or gets himself into situations in which he is likely to suffer injury.

His chances of suffering injury are increased by the fact that his guilty conscience impairs his ability to concentrate. He has trouble not only listening to what others are saying but also paying attention to what he himself is doing.

"Bad company" may be a sign of a guilty conscience. Fear of being discovered forces the person with a guilty conscience to restrict his friendships to a few people, those who don't seem threatening to him. Often, these are people who also have conscience problems. Such persons tend to attract each other for support, but they don't actually support one another. They drag one another down.

Depression often can be traced to a bad conscience. Guilt

burns up emotional energy. It drives the guilty person to
undertake strenuous cover-up activities, none of which ever
yields any reward or sense of fulfillment. These activities
burn up mental and physical energy. When he is emotionally, mentally, and physically exhausted—and has
nothing to show for all of his exertion—the guilty person
plunges to the depths of depression.

A person with a guilty conscience is often accusing and
critical. In an effort to divert attention from his own faults,
he is quick to point out similar faults in others.

When either partner shows several of these characteristics,
the relationship is in trouble. And there's little chance
matters will improve until the Holy Spirit is allowed to do
his cleansing work in the heart of the person with the guilt
problem.

SOLUTION

The basis for a clear conscience is confession and acceptance
of God's promise of forgiveness through Christ's redeeming
death. In dying on the cross, Jesus paid the penalty for your
sins, whatever they are, and for that reason God can justly
forgive you (1 John 1:9).

To confess, though, you may have to do a little work.
You need to be specific in asking forgiveness.

One Christian counselor suggests that you make a list of
people with whom you have problems. Then note beside
each name that person's offenses toward you and your
offenses toward that person.

First, by faith and dependence on the grace of God, forgive
each person of his offenses toward you. Remember, that's the
key to having your own sins forgiven—your ability to
forgive others (Matt. 6:14, 15).

Next, go over the list of offenses you've committed against
others. Decide if any restitution needs to be made, or can be
made. If restitution can be made, do so. If not, simply
depend on the mercy and forgiveness of God to cleanse you
and set matters straight.

Then, if possible, go to the offended one and ask forgiveness. Don't go with the attitude, "I forgive you but I
won't forget," or "I forgive you but it was mostly your fault

or partly your fault." Don't go trying to justify or excuse
your offense. Don't go expecting anything from the person—
a smile, a change of attitude toward you, or any favorable
response. Go knowing full well that he or she may not
forgive you. You are doing the will of God and if the person
does not respond properly, his or her problem will be with
God and not with you.

When you've sincerely confessed and asked forgiveness
both to God and to those whom you've offended, your
conscience will be clear. God will see to that.

PROBLEM: BITTERNESS

Another great enemy sometimes stands between a husband
and wife and the oneness God means for them to enjoy—
bitterness.

Bitterness operates like a dull toothache, gouging away at
marital happiness until the very foundations of the
relationship buckle.

How can you tell when bitterness is a problem in your
date or your marriage partner? It gives itself away in a
number of ways.

Distrust is perhaps the most common evidence observed in
cases of bitterness. If a girl loved a boy in the past and
he walked out on her, leaving her deeply hurt, she may
suffer from the numbing scar tissues of bitterness. The
experience may have left her emotionally incapable of
trusting another boy. Boys can be wounded in the same way.
And when they are, they sometimes bear the marks of
bitterness in the form of suspicion and distrust. Not all
distrust may be traced to bitterness, but often it can be.

Insensitivity may also be an indication of bitterness. Once
hurt, the bitter person constructs a hard shell of resistance
around his feelings. "Nobody's going to hurt me again." But
the shell, rather than offering real protection from hurt,
merely prevents the embittered person's feelings from
reaching out to others.

If the embittered person has been hurt by an authority
figure, he or she may lash out at all authority with vicious
criticism. The caustic tongue serves as a whiplash of
retribution against the offenders.

Tension may suggest the presence of bitterness. When the bitter person thinks of those who hurt him, his muscles grow taut. The effort to harden himself against further hurt produces more tension.

Bitterness sometimes results in ingratitude. The bitter person regards every blessing as compensation for the injury suffered. Nothing can be looked on as a gift to be thankful for, since he considers everything as being owed to him.

The embittered person will sometimes try to hide his problem by flattering those who have done the hurt—or who are imagined to have done it.

Ironically the injured one often falls into a pattern of injuring others. The motive is revenge upon those who have hurt him. But the arrows of his vindictiveness strike many innocent people as he lashes out wildly to avenge his grief.

Self-centeredness becomes a prominent characteristic in the life of the embittered. His hurt, his revenge, protection for his feelings—these take priority in his life. There's no room for service to others.

Bitterness leads finally to depression. The embittered person expends vast amounts of emotional, psychological, and physical energy putting on false fronts, trying to get even, resisting displays of tenderness, doubting and suspecting others. Sooner or later, exhaustion strikes him down.

One of the greatest dangers in bitterness is the fact that it's contagious. Mary marries a boy who had been deeply hurt by someone he trusted. At first she tries to cheer him up. He rejects her sympathy and reacts with annoyance when she interrupts his brooding with words of comfort. Soon she discovers that the only way she can comfort him is by sharing his bitterness toward the one who offended him. Because it comforts him, he stirs up her bitterness until soon it equals his. Two bitter heads are not better than one.

Mary learns this the hard way. Slowly she begins to resent her husband. In her eyes, he has begun to resemble the one who caused his own bitterness, and he has taught her to despise people like that. He reacts by rejecting her because now she is the one who has hurt him. The two are bitter against each other, each blaming the other for robbing the marriage of the happiness and fulfillment it promised. Physical illness often results when bitterness reaches such a depth.

SOLUTION

Bitterness can, and has been, banished from marriages. Those who search the Word of God can find remedies for it.

The basic requirement in getting rid of bitterness is to realize that because you are a child of God, nothing comes upon you that hasn't been filtered through the love of God and his purpose for your life. God's primary purpose for your life, as we discussed earlier, is for you to be conformed to the image of his Son. He wants you to be more and more like Jesus.

Once you accept this truth, you can take a positive attitude toward bitterness, instead of a self-destructive negative attitude. You can see those who offend you as tools of God, working out his purpose in your life, just as Jesus saw those who crucified him and asked God to forgive them (Luke 23:34).

Through the enlightenment of the Scriptures, you can recognize bitterness as a form of vengeance, which God gives his children no right to exercise (Rom. 12:17-20).

You might even come to realize that your bitterness is making you just like the one who has offended you, the one you're bitter against (Rom. 2:1-3).

Romans 8:28 tells us that God works all things together for good for those who love him. Even the offenses that tend to make you bitter can be used of God to work for your good if you'll let them be. In fact, God may have allowed the offenses for the very purpose of working something wonderful in your life that couldn't be accomplished in any other way.

You say, "He lied to my boss and cost me my job—how can God work that for good?" Jesus commanded you to love those who persecute you and despitefully use you. How could you learn to love people like that if no one ever offended you?

It may be that you've suffered some deep tragedy in your life. Maybe your child has been murdered. Surely God couldn't work anything as catastrophic as that for good. Well, he caused the murder of his own child to work for good. He let it stand as the price for your sins and mine, and then he raised him to eternal life. God could use your tragedy to lead you to an understanding of God's love that would surpass anything you could otherwise achieve—if you are willing by faith to let him do so. You may see as few others are ever able to see how much God loved you—and the world—to give his only begotten Son that all who believe in him might not perish but have everlasting life (John 3:16).

What about that person who has offended you repeatedly over a period of months and years? He's cheated you out of the joy of every success you've ever had, and when you've failed he's been right there to rub salt in your wounds. God says we're to love our enemies. How can you learn to love your enemies if you don't have any?

When you can see injuries and offenses as tools in the hand of God working for your good, you can overcome bitterness. You can forgive and be forgiven. You can build in your life a Spirit of forgiveness.

NINE
PURITY

Many marriages fall because they are built on the quicksand of moral impurity. This character flaw appears in both boys and girls but, because of their nature, girls are especially vulnerable to exploitation by boys with impure lifestyles. The pattern may be something like this.

Jerry, a boy controlled by impure motives, dates Jill, a girl who hasn't "been around" a great deal and is still relatively innocent about such things. Jerry heaps praise on Jill because of her apparent purity. He goes out of his way to impress her and win her affections. He puts her on a pedestal and convinces her that he would never, never do anything to harm or displease her. Jerry seems sincere and, from a conscious standpoint, he may be. He simply does not realize the motives for his own behavior.

Because Jerry makes her feel so special, Jill becomes very fond of him. She likes to hear him praise her and tell her how much he loves and adores her. Finally, she becomes convinced that she is "in love" with Jerry and consents to marry him.

In the marriage relationship, Jerry begins to express what he conceives to be "normal" physical love. He expects her to respond with the same ravenous desire for physical gratification.

Jill is hurt, disillusioned, and disappointed. Marriage is not the blissful relationship she expected. Jerry seems to want nothing but satisfaction for his sexual drive, which to Jill seems coarse and revolting. He seems to care little about meeting her needs and shows no sensitivity toward her desires or her concept of what marriage should be like. Sex becomes a meaningless ordeal to her. While she yields outwardly to his advances, she cringes inwardly every time he touches her.

Jill's not fooling Jerry with her facade of cooperation. He detects that inward resistance, and soon he begins to demand genuine response to his advances. Bitter arguments follow, and the resulting unpleasantries inflict severe wounds on the spirit of the marriage.

Jerry begins to feel that Jill is defying his leadership role, as well as rejecting him physically. His ego hungers for something Jill isn't providing—the feeling that he's a "real man," that he's the boss in his house and that he's fulfilling his role as husband in a superior manner. This hunger leads him to admire other women and to begin to wonder if another woman might meet his needs better than Jill.

When Jill notices Jerry's attention straying to other women, jealousy consumes her. She becomes fearful and insecure, sensing that she lacks the ability to meet his physical needs. She doubts her own "womanhood." Still, since sexual relations have become so distasteful to her, she avoids physical involvement. Not only does she find it disgusting but she also equates it with failure and disappointment. She invents ways to spoil his every advance—starting fights, faking illness, planning activities that interfere with sex life.

Determined to light in her the physical appetites that motivate him, Jerry begins to expose Jill to erotic books, magazines, and movies. He thinks she'll react to these sensual materials in the way he does and that she'll begin to fulfill his physical needs. When she reacts with revulsion, he ridicules her for being "abnormal" in her attitudes toward sex.

In an effort to force her to yield to his desires by making her feel guilty, Jerry reveals to their friends that Jill doesn't satisfy him sexually. Jill turns livid with resentment. Her anger turns to bitterness, and when she does get trapped into sexual relations with him, her involvement is purely mechanical.

Finally, the cold truth dawns on Jerry. Jill's never going to satisfy his overdeveloped appetites for sexual gratification. He begins inventing other means to fulfill his physical drives. Some of these may be real and physical. Others may be entirely imagined. In either event, Jerry's mind becomes preoccupied with lustful thoughts and fantasies. He loses his ability to concentrate. Having once made a commitment to Christ and attempted to become a dedicated follower, he now senses a deep and permanent spiritual defeat. He openly excuses and defends his sensual feelings and actions.

Jill also seeks to find fulfillment for her needs apart from the marriage relationship. She looks to other men for the attention and sense of security and self-worth that Jerry no longer provides. As often happens in such cases, Jill becomes emotionally involved with doctors, counselors, and ministers. She seeks counseling—but not to find a solution to her problems. Rather, counseling becomes an end in itself, because it gives her a sympathetic listener and a feeling of importance.

Jerry can be jealous, too—and he is. Seeing her admiration for the men counseling her, he tries to restrict her contacts with them and to discredit them in her eyes.

When Jerry seems to be trying to interfere with her "spiritual life," Jill doubts that he's a Christian. That gives her grounds to begin justifying steps to dissolve the marriage and separate from him permanently.

Jerry becomes bitter toward "religion." If Jill's religious, he says, it's not for him. He renounces belief in God and the Bible. Rather than repent of his impurity, he turns his back on righteousness.

In so doing, he plays into Jill's hands, and she proceeds with her plans for a divorce.

Impurity reveals itself in a number of character defects and behavior patterns.

One of the most common signs of impurity is persistence in distorting or rejecting Biblical precepts. Romans 1:18 says the unrighteous will "hold [or hold down] the truth in unrighteousness," and 2 Timothy 4:3, 4 warns: "For the time will come when they will not endure [accept] sound doctrine; but after their own lusts shall they heap to themselves teachers, having itching ears; and they shall turn away their ears from the truth, and shall be turned unto fables [fictitious teachings]."

Remember, Jerry lost his ability to concentrate when he became preoccupied with impure thoughts and fantasies. That's another indication of impurity—lack of concentration, apparent instability in thought and behavior.

Impure persons also are quick to justify their sensual behavior. They're often supportive of those who are immoral and defensive of their rights to behave as they do. They will certainly defend themselves and justify their actions when criticized or condemned by anyone else.

In many cases, impure persons have carefully worked out philosophies that lend credence to their immorality. The underlying motivation for developing such rationalizations is the immoral persons' self-condemnation. Self can't tolerate condemnation by self. It must devise an elaborate defense for security reasons.

The Bible refers to this as "perverse disputings [misleading arguments] of men of corrupt minds, and destitute of the truth" (1 Tim. 6:5).

Sometimes impure persons strive to ease their consciences by getting feverishly involved in religious or social activities. By "good works," they hope to escape the inner condemnation they feel.

The impure scoff at authority, because authority figures generally act in ways that conflict with their impure lifestyles. The laws and rules necessary for an orderly society forbid many of the activities the impure crave to indulge in, because those activities are socially destructive. They undermine and tear down marriage, the family, the home, orderly behavior—all the mores and institutions that hold society together. Authority figures are charged with enforcing the rules that forbid such behavior. So, naturally, the impure who want to do such things resent authority.

One of the most familiar proverbs says, "as he thinketh in his heart, so is he" (Prov. 23:7). And so are the impure. Their entire lifestyle—their speech, their lewd actions, their lustful stares, the kind of company they enjoy, the books and magazines they read, the kind of entertainment they seek—

points directly to the dangerous flaw they try so assiduously to hide.

STEPS TO A SOLUTION

1. Confess and Repent. The first step to conquering the problem of impurity is the same as that required for freedom from any sin—confession and repentance. And the two always go hand in hand. Without confession there can be no repentance. Confession involves an admission of guilt—first to oneself and then to God. Repentance means a solemn renunciation of the fault that brought on the guilt and a heartfelt resolve to avoid, in the power of God, ever repeating the sinful thought or action again. It's impossible to repent if you haven't first admitted you've done something calling for repentance. It's impossible to confess, in the true sense of the term, without experiencing in your heart a deep intent to repent of the confessed sin.

The word "confess" derives from two words. The two words in English would translate roughly as "agree-speak." To confess, then, means a great deal more than just to admit that you've done something—or haven't done something. It means to agree with God in what he says about the thing confessed. If God says the act or thought is sinful, you agree with God that it's sinful. God says sin, any sin, merits the death penalty. "The soul that sinneth, it shall die" (Ezek. 18:4). You agree that your thought or act merits the death penalty, that you really deserve to die because you've disobeyed God and brought dishonor on his holy name and grief and distress to your friend or family or neighbor.

Once you've thoroughly visualized the consequences of your sin, both to your relationship to God and to others, and have acknowledged that you deserve death for the sin, then you let the Holy Spirit show you the root sin, the underlying cause of the thought or action that offended God and others. That root cause is always the same, but you must identify it and confess it every time you're convicted of any sin. One sin is the father of all sin, and it must continually be confessed and repented of.

That root sin is not allowing Jesus to be Lord of your life.

You may have heard the saying, "If Jesus isn't Lord of all, then he isn't Lord at all." That's a hard saying. But as I grow in my own Christian experience, and as I hear the testimonies of others committed to walking with the Lord, I become more and more convinced that it's absolutely true.

When we come to Jesus Christ for foregiveness of our sins and his precious gift of eternal life, bought with his blood at Calvary, he demands to be Lord of all—to have complete control of our lives. If we don't give him complete mastery over our lives, he allows things to happen to us. He lets the pressures build until something has to give. Either we awaken and repent and give him control of our lives—completely—or he breaks us.

Of course, when we come to God in confession and repentance, he forgives us and cleanses us from all unrighteousness (1 John 1:9). But too many Christians claim that verse too lightly. That verse packs a wallop of truth that we don't dare attempt to brush aside.

First, it contains that double-edged word "confess" which, as I've already explained, carries with it not only the idea of acknowledging a sin but sensing revulsion toward that sin and an overwhelming determination to turn from it forever.

Next, the verse contains the precious promise that if we confess in this true meaning of the word, God "is faithful and just to forgive us our sins and to cleanse us from all unrighteousness." But don't skim over that promise, in your confessions, without taking note of the grounds on which it is made.

God can promise to forgive us our sins, and do so justly, only because of the finished work of Jesus Christ. Your sin warrants the death penalty, remember. To fulfill the law of God, that penalty has to be paid. But, praise God, Jesus paid it for you on the cross. His death, and that alone, enables God to be faithful in his promise to forgive you. Otherwise, he could not do so and remain true to his just and righteous character.

Only when you've recognized that you've sinned, agreed with God concerning the consequences, realized that that sin caused Jesus Christ to die an agonizing death on the cross, turned from the sin in revulsion and a sincere prayer for power to avoid it forever and giving Christ total control of your life—

only when you've confessed in that manner have you practiced complete repentance.

Complete repentance, in just that manner, is the only path to freedom from life-wrecking, marriage-rending, happiness-robbing impurity.

2. Walk in the Spirit. The second step to being rid of impurity is to begin learning to walk in the Spirit of God. Among God's most beautiful promises is the one found in Galatians 5:16: "This I say then, Walk in the Spirit, and ye shall not fulfill the lust of the flesh." There's hope for you if your problem is one of impurity. You don't have to try to justify it with the lie given you by the world and the Devil which says, "Don't worry about it . . . just give in to it . . . it's only natural," knowing all the time that it's leading you deeper and deeper into guilt and agony. You don't have to give in. You only have to obey God's commandment to walk in the Spirit, and he takes care of the rest. He sees to it, according to the promise of his word, that you will *not* "be continually plotting and striving to fulfill lustful physical appetites" [my paraphrase].

How do we walk in the Spirit, then? To "walk" simply means to live life one step at a time. That's the first thing God wants us to understand about the Christian life. We don't say "Abracadabra!" and get a perfect, sinless life handed to us for as long as we're in this world. We live, as the song says, "one day at a time"—more accurately one breath or one heartbeat at a time. To walk in the Spirit means, first of all, to live life step by step in complete dependence on the Holy Spirit—for wisdom, guidance, strength and victory.

Before we can walk in the Spirit, though, we've got to be sure we understand some basic truths.

—The Holy Spirit, the Father and Jesus Christ are one, in the wonderful mystery of the Trinity. When you received Jesus Christ as your personal Savior—assuming that you have—he entered your life to live in you by his Holy Spirit. Your life became the temple of the Holy Spirit (1 Cor. 3:16). You have God, Jesus Christ, living in you.

—God is not content merely to have his Spirit residing in you, though. He insists that his Spirit fill every compartment of your personality, control every aspect of your life—your mind, your will, your emotions (Eph. 5:18).

—As he lives in us, the Holy Spirit brings to our attention thoughts, words, and actions that dishonor God. What we do is our choice. If we follow these thoughts and actions, we behave impurely. This grieves the Holy Spirit—it distresses and dismays him (Eph. 4:30). But if we give the undesirable thoughts and actions over to the Holy Spirit to be "mortified" (put to death), then we are walking in the Spirit (Rom. 8:13).

The way to be sure we're getting the Holy Spirit's messages about all our thoughts and actions is to fill our minds with the Word of God. The Holy Spirit uses God's Word as a weapon to defend us, just as Jesus used it to ward off the temptations of Satan in the wilderness. Psalm 119:11 makes it plain that the only way we can live a pure life is to hide God's Word in our heart that we might not sin against him.

As we walk in this manner, giving over to the Holy Spirit for destruction of the things that displease him and trusting him for guidance and power, our spiritual legs increase in strength. In time, the walk becomes more "natural" for us. But let me warn you that it never becomes easy. God tends to work with us as a weight lifting coach works with his athletes. He makes us stronger by increasing our burdens.

Yet remember his promise: "Ye shall find rest unto your souls, for my yoke is easy and my burden is light" (Matt. 11:29, 30). The difficult part is to develop the practice of yielding every step to the Holy Spirit. Once we've done that, the walk itself requires no effort at all on our part. The Holy Spirit walks for us.

One final word on walking in the Spirit. The physical appetites (which are not wrong in themselves) and the distractions of the world raise up hindrances to walking in the Spirit. Of course, we know not to "love the things of the world." But sometimes we have to go farther if we want to sharpen our spiritual sensitivity. We have to actually withdraw for a period and even deny our bodies the physical food they desire. Fasting is a biblical principle too few Christians practice in attaining spiritual growth. It should be practiced carefully, though, and not in a way that could damage physical health. And it should be done only as the Holy Spirit impresses us to do so. If we fast from the wrong motives or for the wrong purposes, God will not honor it and it may actually result in a spiritual setback. Done properly and at the Spirit's prompting, it can be a tremendous blessing.

Finally, God directs us to combat impurity by "the renewing of your minds" (Rom. 12:2). We can let God transform our thought-lives by hiding his Word in our hearts through memorizing Scripture (Psa. 119:11). If our minds are filled with God's Word, the Devil finds it hard to get a word in edgewise.

We can also help renew our minds by visualizing the Word of God, that is, picturing in our minds how it applies to real-life situations.

Most important of all, we can renew our minds by actualizing God's Word—that is, by acting out at every opportunity the principles we've pictured in our minds.

Have you ever heard the expression, "I just can't see myself doing a thing like that"? Well, practice seeing yourself doing the things that please God—then go out and do them in the wisdom and power of the Spirit.

That's walking in the Spirit. That's victory over impurity!

TEN
AWARENESS OF PURPOSE

A person who doesn't know the purpose of life is like a jetliner roaming the stratosphere without a destination. He will drift aimlessly, or choose first one compass heading and then another, without ever getting anywhere. And he'll wind up out of fuel, and perhaps in wreckage.

SIGNS OF A PROBLEM

Several characteristics flash like neon signs in the personality of someone who lacks awareness of purpose, making this one of the easiest problems to spot.

The most obvious indication of purposelessness, of course, is simple indecision. If you know what your purpose in life is, you know where you're going and what it takes to get there. You have some goals. To reach those goals, you know there are certain steps you must take and certain hindrances you must overcome or avoid. This knowledge gives you a basis for making decisions. A choice confronts you and you say, almost without hesitation, "I'll go this way—to go the other way would take me off the course to my goal." If you have no goals, though, you have no basis for deciding which choice is the better for you. There are no guidelines, no criteria, for making a wise selection. So you're wishy-washy. You flounder in indecision.

Disorganization is another trademark of purposelessness. Lacking firm goals, someone without purpose in life can't set up an effective system of priorities. What to do first, second, and third? What to devote great effort to and what to take in stride? What to invest much time in, and what to give "a lick and a promise?" Those are questions the purposeless person never seems to answer correctly. Again, the reason is simple. How can he know how to spend his time and energy if he doesn't know what he's trying to buy with them?

Purposeless persons are often lethargic and lazy. You couldn't get them to move if they were sitting on an ant bed. Purpose is an energizing force. When you're going somewhere that you want to go, you're eager to get there in the shortest time possible. When you don't know where you're going, or whether you really want to go, you don't have any incentive to get up and move out. Indolence is one of the surest signs of lack of purpose.

Boredom is another. If you've got a goal, progress toward that goal brings satisfaction, elation. You've cleared a couple of hurdles. Only X-number still to go. But if you've got no purpose, nothing gives you a sense of achievement. You may have done something quite admirable. But if it doesn't move you closer to your ultimate objective, even the most brilliant feat won't excite you. It will be meaningless.

The constant companion of boredom is complaining. If nothing ever gives you satisfaction or fulfillment, everything soon begins to get on your nerves. You blame the people and conditions around you for your misery and emptiness.

Fear also is many times an indicator of purposelessness. The person whose reason for living is clearly defined keeps his eye on the goals. He's too intent, too preoccupied with doing what he knows to do and enjoys, to think about failure. In a car traveling over a narrow mountain road, the driver is likely to be the least nervous occupant. He knows where he's going. He's got control of things. If the one with purpose does fail, he immediately picks himself up and starts out anew toward his goal. The thing he is doing is not an end in itself. To someone without purpose, whatever he's doing at the moment is the only thing in sight. To fail at that is to lose all.

Fear of failure, of course, breeds another sign of

purposelessness: insecurity. If your immediate circumstances
are all you can count on, and you know how easily
circumstances can change, you're going to feel about as secure
as a wounded mosquito in a pond full of bullfrogs.

One who is purposeless will often show other characteristics—a tendency to squander time, energy, and resources on
things of no enduring value, and an insatiable appetite for
escapist entertainment and pleasant diversions.

These tendencies sometimes lead to entrapment in sex sin,
alcoholism, and drug addiction.

If purposeless persons can be successful in practically nothing
in life, then certainly they're not likely to be successful in a
relationship as demanding as marriage.

Joe married Phyllis, a beautiful girl but one who had no
clear idea about life's purpose. Joe was an achiever, a real go-
getter. He was rising fast in his career. He was a good husband
and father. He needed a wife who could assume responsibilities
with the home and children.

Phyllis didn't fill the bill. Interested only in her own immediate needs and circumstances, she didn't plan anything—
not even the evening meals. Once in a while she made a stab at
cleaning house and doing the laundry. But she was easily dis-
couraged. She couldn't make decisions even about things like
buying clothes for herself and the children. She became frumpy
and unattractive.

Concerned about his once lovely wife, Joe began to push her
to tidy things up. She resented the pressure. It reminded her of
her mother, who used to do everything around the house and
make all the decisions, then scold her for her slothfulness. She
began to feel the same hostility toward Joe that she used to feel
toward her mother.

Joe soon realized that Phyllis' lack of purpose and
indecisiveness was letting his home fall apart. It was rubbing
off on the kids, making them lethargic and sulky, and
hindering him in his work. He still loved Phyllis, but he
couldn't entirely fight off the bitterness he felt. He was only
human, and he had needs that an uncaring, unkempt wife
simply wasn't able or willing to meet.

Phyllis wanted Joe to accept and adore her as he once did.
To win his favor, she invented all kinds of excuses for

behaving as she did. She hinted that she might not be
physically healthy. But for the most part she blamed other
people and circumstances. She constantly ran down the
neighbors, the church, the government.

After many months of trying to get Phyllis to change, Joe
gave up. He began to stay away from home a good deal, to
work late at night, to seize opportunities for out of town travel.
He started yearning for the companionship of another woman.

Now with the hurt of neglect heaped upon her other
problems, Phyllis withdrew into the only security she could
find—the walls of her own home and an almost endless series
of escapist television programs and plotless novels.

The marriage had been damaged, almost certainly to an
irreparable degree, by the problem of purposelessness.

SOLUTION

As we have seen, the problem of a lack of a sense of purpose
must be corrected—the earlier in a relationship, the better. A
sense of purpose can be developed by following God's
leadership.

Of course, the Bible doesn't say what every individual's
specific purpose should be. But it does tell what everyone's
general purpose should be and, once that is understood, the
specific purpose usually reveals itself in time.

The ultimate purpose of every Christian's life is to achieve
the full potential planned for him or her by God. Remember
Romans 8:29, where Paul defines that purpose as being
"conformed to the image of his Son." In other words, we're to
be Christlike. But being Christlike involves other people. It
includes the further objective of developing Christlikeness in
others. Paul speaks of this aspect of being Christlike, too: "My
little children, of whom I travail in birth again until Christ be
formed in you . . ." (Gal. 4:19).

It follows then that, whatever God's specific purpose for you
may be, God's general purpose involves you in relationship
with other people. It involves both leading others to become
Christians and helping Christians become spiritually mature.
Your particular purpose probably calls for you to concentrate
more on one aspect of the overall purpose than the other—to

emphasize winning the lost or maturing the saved. The spiritual gifts and the circumstances in which God places you at a given time may help you determine which aspect to give the most attention to.

Pursuing God's general purpose affords the most stimulating and fulfilling lifestyle imaginable. It requires, first of all, a close and constant relationship between you and your heavenly Father. That in itself is the essence of eternal life (John 17:3). It requires diligence in learning and preparing yourself, and those activities are a delight (Psa. 119:24).

Problems, conflicts, and challenges will be encountered along the route to fulfilling this general purpose for your life—the purpose of developing Christlikeness in yourself and others. But through the eyes of the Holy Spirit, who will be your fellow traveler every step of the way, these obstacles will no longer appear to be threats to your security. Instead, you'll see them as opportunities for God to demonstrate his wisdom and power and opportunities for you to learn and grow spiritually.

You'll doubtlessly have disappointments and failures. But if you keep your eye on your goal—which is the fullness of Christ—you can regard these as learning experiences preparing you for greater enjoyment of your next victory—which, you can be sure, won't be long in coming.

The spirit, the enthusiasm, the strength, and stability that you develop in pursuing God's general purpose will carry over and benefit you in whatever your specific purpose may be.

You may not be what the world terms a great success—someone immersed in material abundance. But you will be a success in the things that really matter, the things that are important to God, fulfilling to you, and profitable to others. And God promises that this is sufficient for a life of joy.

Blessed is the man, the woman, the marriage in which both are aware of God's purpose for their lives and both are pursuing that purpose.

ELEVEN
FINANCIAL RESPONSIBILITY

Bill and Jan are a typical, modern couple. Though both
profess to be Christians, they've fallen for some of the world's
philosophies and lifestyles. They've swallowed the line that
marriage is a fifty-fifty proposition, a partnership. They've
shoved aside as old-fashioned the Biblical principles for
marriage and the division of marital responsibilities set up in
the Scriptures.

Both know when they decide to get married that Bill can't
support the two of them with his income alone. He still has
some schooling to complete, and he's at the bottom of the
ladder with his company. But so what? Both partners have to
work in order to make it in nearly every marriage these days,
don't they? Jan agrees even before the wedding to work until
Bill finishes school and gets well established in his career.
Later on, she'll drop out of the business world and they'll
begin their family.

In depending on his wife for part of the basic support of the
household, though, Bill has made a serious mistake. He has
surrendered a part of the responsibility that God in his plan
for marriage has assigned to the husband.

Let me pause here to explain this principle of financial
responsibility, because it's one of the most misunderstood and
disregarded of all the biblical tenets on marriage. It's not
wrong in itself for Jan to work outside the home. What made

it a mistake in Bill and Jan's case is that the marriage depended financially from its inception on her working. If Jan wanted to work outside the home before they had children, that would have done no harm, provided certain other scriptural guidelines were followed. If Bill became disabled, or other financial tragedies struck forcing Jan to provide part of the basic income, that, too, would be another story. But any couple courts marital disaster if they disregard the principle that the husband is responsible for supporting the family merely because they do not have the patience to wait until he is able to fulfill that responsibility. God says, "wait on the Lord." He despises impatience with his order of things, and those who run ahead of his timetable do so at great peril.

The danger soon became apparent in the household of Bill and Jan. When he gave up some of his role in providing financially for the family, he unknowingly surrendered some of his authority over financial matters, also. Jan begins to use much of the money she earns, not for basic financial needs, but for expenditures that express her personality and natural feminine inclinations. She starts buying things to decorate and beautify the home. Every item bought for the home seems to lead to something else. A table calls for a lamp. A picture calls for a mirror. New curtains call for new bedspreads. There seems no end to the list of things that would make the home just what Jan would like it to be.

Meanwhile, Bill begins to run into trouble with his bank balance. He discovers what so many young husbands quickly realize—that his estimates of what it costs to support a wife and a home were miserably below actual costs. He didn't figure on Jan's big dental bills or the car needing an overhaul after only 50,000 miles or the plumber having to replace a sewer line to the ten-year-old house they had bought.

Bill and Jan were like what someone has described the typical American family to be—they've had an unexpected expenditure every month for the last six months but are not expecting one this month.

Just when the pressure gets so strong that Bill's wondering if he'll ever see light at the end of his financial tunnel, Jan begins to show signs of wear. She's physically run down from trying to take care of the house, the laundry, and the meals while holding down a full-time job. Since she's working her fingers to the bone to help support the family, she doesn't see why he can't pitch in with the household chores. That's how all the modern sociologists say it should be.

But Bill doesn't see things as the women's liberation groups see them. He's doing his part, trying to stay sharp and advance in his job and burning the midnight oil on courses that will boost his career in the years ahead. He thinks Jan should show the physical stamina he displays. It's the least she can do, if she expects him to have the freedom he needs to complete his education and get somewhere on the job.

Bill's attitude hardens Jan's determination to have some say in how money she earns is spent. Now she resents it openly when Bill calls on her to pay a pressing or unexpected bill, and she really blows up if he spends a nickel on something she doesn't regard as absolutely essential.

This stirs resistance in Bill to what he interprets as a defiant streak in Jan. She seems to be trying to take over control of household finances, and Bill instinctively senses that's not how things ought to be.

If she wants to run things, though, Bill will fix that. He'll just let her take over a chore he's never really enjoyed anway— the paying of the bills. But Bill can't just turn *everything* over to her. He insists on continuing to spend money for things he thinks are necessary, often without even consulting Jan. This makes her bill-paying chore an impossible ordeal.

Then another problem Bill and Jan didn't foresee begins to complicate their lives. She begins to want children. Her desire increases as the months and years flick by and she realizes the childbearing period of her life is slipping away. She also realizes, however, that she can't have children because they can't live without the income from her job. With that thought nagging at her, Jan begins to nag Bill. "Can't you get a better paying job—or take on an extra job for a while—so I can quit work and have a baby?"

Bill wants a family, too, so Jan's arguments finally hit a responsive chord in his masculine heart. He takes on a "moonlighting" job, in addition to his regular work.

This enables Jan to have a baby, but the price is high. Bill just can't work two jobs, handle the financial pressures that are piling up on him, and meet his other responsibilities as a husband. Those "other responsibilities" include many things that can't be measured in dollars and cents but are far more valuable than money—things like giving Jan emotional support by reassuring her when she's down, expressing appreciation for her, providing spiritual leadership, being a good listener when she's telling him the troubles of the day, tending to home repairs and other chores when they need to be done, or just telling her verbally that he loves her.

On top of the emotional deprivation Jan feels during the period in which she is bearing two children, she takes on guilt feelings when she goes back to work. She really wants to be with the children. She feels that they need her special love and care. When she leaves them at the child-care center, they often cry. Those wails of "Mommie, please don't leave me again, please take me with you" haunt her through the day.

Soon, Jan begins to try to appease her guilt feelings by showering her children with attention and material things when she's with them. Though her working requires extra money for child care, clothes, transportation, income taxes and eating out, she spends even more indulging the kids because of her guilty conscience.

While he wanted kids, Bill didn't bargain for this. Even working two jobs, he's finding it harder than ever to make ends meet. Not only that, but the kids interfere with his work, his study, and sometimes his sleep. He lets Jan know they're her responsibility. She's not only to take care of their needs but also keep them quiet when he's trying to work or get some rest.

Unwittingly, Bill merely drives Jan in the direction she was already headed—toward transferring her love to the children. Soon he senses that his own emotional and physical needs aren't being met. A feeling of isolation and rejection closes in on him like the jaws of a vise.

An ego like Bill's doesn't let itself be crushed without a fight. He begins to build a defense of cold resentment.

His resentment meets with bitterness in Jan, and her bitterness begets bitterness in him. Soon the life of Bill and Jan becomes an endless cycle of tension, quarreling, resentment, bitterness, physical and emotional exhaustion, spiritual deprivation, and deep insecurity.

Their marriage isn't yet beyond repair, but mending it will require drastic changes in attitudes and behavior patterns. Only the hand of the Lord, reshaping and remolding the hearts of two spiritually crippled adults, could work such a dramatic transformation.

And the transforming work had better come quickly, because in the present situation lasting damage is being inflicted not only on Bill and Jan but on their children—and their children's children, to the third and fourth generation.

What Scriptures set forth the principles violated by Bill and Jan? Innumerable ones. But the basic violations go against such verses as these:

"But if any provide not for his own, and specially for those of his own house, he hath denied the faith, and is worse than an infidel [unbeliever]" (1 Tim. 5:8).

"Likewise, ye husbands, dwell with them [your wives] according to knowledge [with intelligence], giving honor unto the wife, as unto the weaker vessel, and as being heirs together of the grace of life . . ." (1 Pet. 3:7)

"Better is little with the fear of the Lord than great treasure and trouble therewith" (Prov. 15:16).

"Wives, submit yourselves unto your own husbands, as unto the Lord. For the husband is the head of the wife, even as Christ is the head of the church . . ." (Eph. 5:22, 23).

"Husbands, love your wives, even as Christ also loved the church, and gave himself for it" (Eph. 5:25).

These precepts may seem quaint and outdated amid all the modern sociological and psychological theorizing about marriage, but God is not mocked (Gal. 6:7). His principles can no more be ignored without disaster than can the physical laws that govern the universe. Yet millions of intelligent couples who wouldn't think of stepping out of an airplane without a parachute take equally suicidal chances with their marriages, seemingly without a second thought. No wonder some knowledgeable observers are wondering whether the family will survive the close of the twentieth century.

Lack of a healthy sense of financial responsibility is one of the most serious of all threats to a lasting and happy marriage. If either the husband or wife fails to see and fulfill this responsibility in God's way, real oneness will elude the relationship like the pea in the age-old shell game. They may be sure it's here, they may grab for it there. But it won't be found. Marriage counselors everywhere will tell you that "money problems" rank among the leading causes of marital discord and divorce.

SIGNS OF THE PROBLEM

Fortunately a weak sense of financial responsibility, at least on the part of the man, is fairly easy to detect.

It reveals itself in one very obvious way—debt. The financially irresponsible person wants just as many fun things and creature comforts as anyone else. He seldom can pay for things at the time when he wants them so he goes into debt for them without thinking about how he will get the money to pay when the bills come due. Usually, he doesn't have the money at bill time. The unpaid debts pile up. Soon, almost every penny he earns is owed before he receives it. This leads to endless bill juggling and refinancing and borrowing at usurious interest rates, all of which only adds to the problem.

If a young man seems to be head-over-heels in love, check to see if he is also head-over-heels in debt, young woman, before you commit yourself to marry him. If he is, it's apparent that he has the problem of financial irresponsibility.

The problem reveals itself in more subtle ways, too.

Often, an obsession for possessions indicates financial irresponsibility. The desire to own things overpowers the desire to do things God's way. It even outweighs the desire to preserve a good name and reputation. This sign of financial irresponsibility is not restricted to men. It is also common among young women, although at marriageable age most young women have had little opportunity to get into debt.

Both men and women sometimes betray financial irresponsibility through a something-for-nothing attitude. These are the people who are always looking for get-rich-quick schemes that yield financial gains far beyond the work and planning invested. They're forever being misled into unwise investments by amazing success stories that tell only of the gold found at the end of the rainbow, not the effort and skill that went into discovering it.

Lack of savings and investment plans also marks a person as one who is weak in financial responsibility. Rainy days will come. The financially responsible person will prepare by putting something aside for them.

Related to this sign is a fatalistic attitude concerning financial planning. Because the family nest egg has been wiped out three months in a row by unexpected expenses, the husband says "what's the use" and stops trying to save. Or the wife with the insatiable desire for new clothes or things for the house looks at the family income, sees that only a little can be saved out of each paycheck and decides it would be just as well to save nothing.

These are dangerous attitudes. The husband should be asked what he would have used to pay the unexpected expense if he hadn't had the savings. And the wife should be admonished that, no, indeed it's not just as well to save nothing as to save a little.

In saying "take no thought for tomorrow," Jesus wasn't saying not to be frugal in planning financially for the future. He meant only that we should not let our days be burdened with worry and fretting. Failure to plan and save soundly is one of the surest ways to bring about worry and anxiety.

Finally, a young man telegraphs a weak sense of financial responsibility when, like Bill, the husband mentioned earlier, he expects his wife to work to pay basic living expenses. He subtly, perhaps imperceptibly, undermines his wife's respect for him. More seriously, he displeases God by dodging a responsibility God assigned to the husband.

If you look carefully at your own life, or that of the person you're considering marrying, you may see reflections of Bill and Jan or some traces of the warning signs of financial irresponsibility. If so, the problem should be treated by firm adherence to God's principles. Disaster is at the door of your relationship.

STEPS TO A SOLUTION

Many immature young persons consider financial responsibility to be a drag—a set of rules that bind them and keep them from enjoying life. Just the opposite is true. Financial discipline frees a couple to have of what they need and want and to enjoy more of what they have.

If you've ever bought anything on the installment plan, you know it's hard to enjoy something that brings you an unpleasant monthly reminder that you don't really own it.

Getting out of debt should be your first goal if you haven't been following the rules of financial responsibility.

The next goal should be to establish a savings plan. You should be free not only from a burden of debt but also from anxiety over unexpected expenses.

Then get your priorities in the right order concerning what is really important in life. Jesus stated the correct priority in Matthew 6:33 when he said: "But seek ye first the kingdom of God, and his righteousness; and all these [material] things shall be added unto you." He also warned that "a man's life consisteth not in the abundance of the things which he possesseth" (Luke 12:15).

Stop thinking about things on the earth and set your sights on things above, where Christ sits at the right hand of God (Col. 3:1). Forget about how to get rich quick and realize how you can be rich forever. In Christ, you have all that pertains to life and godliness (2 Pet. 1:3).

The Bible spells out plainly the principles that form the foundations for financial responsibility. The basic ingredient is, paradoxical as it may seem, the principle of giving.

God reveals that principle in Malachi 3:10, where he promises that if we give our tithes and offerings to him, he will reward us with more than we are able to receive. Again in Proverbs 19:17, God promises to repay in his undiminishing currency what we give in caring for the poor. In Romans 12:13, he promises to reward us for giving to meet the needs of our brothers and sisters in the faith. And in Luke 6:38, he reveals the marvelous truth that giving results in receiving: "Give and it shall be given unto you . . ."

Another ingredient in God's foundation for financial

responsibility is receiving. We're promised that we will receive
for diligent work (Rom. 12:11) and resourcefulness (Prov.
31:13). The greatest and most reliable avenue for receiving,
however, is one that few Christians utilize to the fullest, and
that is prayer. God promises to give "whatsoever ye shall ask
in prayer" (Matt. 21:22).

The conditions are that we ask on the basis of our
acceptance of Jesus Christ as Savior and Lord, that we ask
believing that we shall receive, and that we ask according to
God's will and not to gratify our own lusts. In response to that
kind of prayer, the Bible says, God is able to do abundantly
above all that we could ask or think (Eph. 3:20).

Spending is the third ingredient in the foundations for
financial responsibility.

It's amazing how specific God is in his instructions if we
would only search them out and take them seriously. On
spending, for instance, God counsels us to build up a strong
sales resistance (Prov. 20:14), shop for the best bargains (Prov.
31:16) and be prompt in meeting financial obligations (Prov.
3:28).

One nationally known Bible teacher and Christian counselor
suggests a series of steps to establishing financial responsibility.
Many couples have followed these steps out of financial
bondage and into financial freedom. Here, in abbreviated form,
are the steps he recommends:

1. Commitment. Recognize God's Word as the final authority
in all financial matters.
Projects. Dedicate to God all your money, possessions, time,
and earning power. Ask him to give you time to consult with
him and his Word when others ask you for money.

2. Commitment. Establish the tithe as an expression of
worship and a regular reminder that all you have belongs to
God. Assume responsibility for the Lord's work through
support of a church in harmony with the Scripture, Christians
in effective ministries, widows and children in distress, the
poor who are unable to provide the necessities of life.
Projects. Use this guide to determine God's will in giving the
tithe:

—Is the work communicating the true message of Scripture?
—Are the people responding positively to the message?
—Are the leaders illustrating Scripture by their lives?
—Is the character of Christ being reproduced?
—Is the work operated efficiently, avoiding waste?

3. Commitment. Evaluate each expenditure on the basis of
how much it will aid in developing spiritual maturity.
Project. Before buying anything, ask yourself:
—Will this make me more effective in witnessing?
—Will it benefit the Lord's reputation?
—Will it increase my love for Christ?
—Has the Lord provided the money for it?

4. Commitment. Establish a timetable for getting out of debt.
Project. Resolve to follow these steps:
—List all debts on items that depreciate in value.
—List all regular expenditures.
—Discontinue or reduce as many expenditures as possible.
—Sell items no longer being used.
—Start paying cash for things you buy.
—Replace high depreciation items, such as a new car.
—Be wise, seek counsel in supplementing income.
—Make any necessary restitution.

5. Commitment. Resolve not to borrow or lend money for
depreciating items.
Project. Review scriptural reasons for not borrowing:
Romans 13:8   Proverbs 22:7   James 4:13-17
1 Timothy 5:8   2 Corinthians 9:11   1 Timothy 6:9-10
Review scriptural reasons for not cosigning notes:
Proverbs 6:1-3; 11:15; 17:18; 20:16; 22:26; 27:13

6. Commitment. Give God an opportunity to demonstrate his
love and power by providing an item before you buy it. (Pray
for it.)
Project. Determine how long you can wait before the item is
needed. Commit the need to God and allow him to provide it
in ordinary or extraordinary ways. Begin a special fund for the
purchase of the needed item.

7. Commitment. Develop sales resistance and the habit of finding best buys.
Project. Before every purchase, ask yourself:
—Do I really need it?
—Am I buying more than I need?
—Does it do what it claims to do?
—Does my use justify purchase or rental?
—Can I avoid paying middlemen?

8. Commitment. Learn home maintenance skills.
Project. Acquire basic skills of carpentry, electrical work and plumbing.

When professional repairs are necessary, turn them into learning sessions for you and your children.

9. Commitment. Evaluate reasons for shortage of funds for needed items.
Projects. When funds are lacking ask:
—Do I really need it?
—Is God testing my faith?
—Have I violated financial principles (see Scriptures above)?
—Have I misspent money?
—Is God indicating a major change in location, vocation or method of service?

Just making that first and second commitment—acknowledging the Word of God as the final authority in financial matters and beginning to tithe as a form of worship and a reminder that God owns it all—can work wonders for your financial problems.

Think of the burden of worry and responsibility it lifts from your shoulders when you acknowledge God's rightful ownership of everything in your possession.

When you have car trouble, you can look up and say, "Lord, your car's acting up. What are you going to do about it?" When the washing machine refuses to spin with a load of wet clothes in it, you can say, "Lord, your machine's on the blink again. Let me know how you want to get it fixed."

That may sound a little facetious. But God promises to answer just such prayers—and he does. He doesn't want anxiety over material things to rob you of your joy. He doesn't want you to worry and fret to the point that your marriage is threatened.

Remember, too, that God owns not only all that you possess but the whole material universe. He has every resource at his command.

That's important to keep in mind when contemplating the sixth step—that of developing the habit of giving God a chance to provide what you need before rushing out to buy it—certainly before rushing out to "charge it." It's amazing how many things God will provide for you without depleting your bank account when you just let him know your need and trust him to supply it.

A friend of mine had one of his cars stolen off a downtown street while he was at work. It was an older model, and he didn't carry theft insurance on it. He had to have the car. His wife needed the family car, and he had no way to get to work. He couldn't imagine how he could buy a car at that point, though, because he had a large family to support and a daughter entering college that year. In fact, he had been praying for the Lord to provide a good used car for his daughter, who would need one since she would be attending college in another city.

When he realized he suddenly had one less car, instead of one more, as he had prayed, he was puzzled. But then he prayed: "Well, Lord, you know my needs. If I need one less car, instead of one more, thank you for letting this happen."

The next evening his father-in-law called long distance from his home in another city. He knew nothing about my friend's problem. My friend was overwhelmed when he heard him say: "Could you use a good car? I'm trading for a new one and they want me to give my old one to them. I'd rather give it to you."

So, in his own way, God had replaced the stolen car with a better car—without cost to my friend.

But that isn't the end of the story. Three weeks later, my friend got a call from the local police department. His stolen car had been recovered. It was intact, except for a dead battery.

For the price of a standard battery and a token payment for

his father-in-law's car to satisfy title transfer requirements my friend had the additional car he had prayed for! That's quite a bargain!

However, God doesn't honor reckless handling of his possessions. He expects us to be good stewards of all that he entrusts to us.

So it's most important that we follow the sound money management steps set forth in Scripture and outlined above. If you or your mate or prospective mate are not following these steps, you're financially irresponsible. You're risking your future security and happiness. You're endangering your marriage.

Make the commitments suggested right now and start ordering your finances according to God's plan. Trust him to honor it and provide the necessary discipline. You'll see a remarkable difference in your money matters. Not only that, you'll see a surprising change in your own outlook on life and in all your relations with others, especially those closest to you.

One other point concerning financial responsibility—and don't think it unimportant because I've left it for last—is that a husband and wife are one in money matters just as they are in all other things. They should plan and handle financial responsibility together. The same applies to a young man and young woman during their engagement.

The basic principle involved in this aspect of oneness is that most marital problems can be avoided if the husband and wife—or the engagement partners—talk things over and come to agreement before decisions are made.

Men and women react to crises and problems differently. Generally, the woman reacts according to immediate needs. The husband almost always reacts in terms of future expectations and what he thinks best for the family in the long run. In discussing a given problem, both have important responsibilities. She must explain her reaction, her concern for emotional needs that should be met immediately. He should clarify the future expectations through which he believes the needs will be met.

Sometimes there may still be disagreement. In such cases, the wife's responsibility is to yield to the husband. He must have the last word on the decision—and assume responsibility for the consequences.

The wife, having done her part, can then trust God in the situation. If her husband proves to be right, she will benefit more than she would have if she had had her way. If he proves wrong, after disregarding her view, she can rest assured that God will teach him a lesson of eternal value in the situation. And she still will benefit!

Meanwhile, her peace and confidence will be a blessing to her husband and the entire family. If she had resented her husband's decision, wrong or right, it would have affected the atmosphere of the home, making a bad situation worse.

The two shall be one flesh. And that oneness is no more important in any aspect of marriage than in the handling of money matters.

PART THREE

THE
RIGHT
SPIRIT

INTRODUCTION

The final thoughts of the chapter on financial responsibility can be expanded in their application to take in most other areas of the husband-wife relationship.

Whatever the feminists or other political pressure groups may say to the contrary, men and women *are* different. They differ not only physically but in the way they approach problems and life in general. Their thought processes simply do not follow the same set of tracks. Both partners should understand the fundamental truth that God did not create man and woman alike. That understanding can spare couples much misery and disappointment. Failure of one or both partners to understand this simple truth can lead to much confusion and unhappiness.

TWELVE
A FAMILIAR PATTERN

The course of events usually follows a pattern something like this:

Paul and Della are a struggling young couple with two preschool children. One day Paul comes home beaming. He's been promoted at the office. It means a raise in pay, which they could certainly use, and a necessary step up the company ladder to future advancement. But it also means that Paul will have to travel quite a lot. Though he'll be home most weekends, Della will have the house and kids to herself nearly all week long.

Della lights up with excitement on first hearing the news, sharing with Paul the joy of his progress. Then, as they discuss it further, she turns strangely morose. Paul hardly notices, but Della's eyes are brimming with tears. She realizes something's wrong. She should be bubbling over with enthusiasm for Paul's new challenge, just as he is. But instead she finds an indescribable sadness washing over her. Fight it as she will, she can't suppress this sadness and join Paul wholeheartedly in his elation.

What Della doesn't realize, and Paul in no way suspects, is that the two are viewing this change in their situation from different perspectives. She's reacting to it from her position and responsibility as a wife and a mother, he from his role and duty as husband and father.

As a wife and mother, Della tends to respond to every situation from the standpoint of immediate needs. She also tends to react more on the basis of emotion than pure logic. For that reason, after the news of Paul's promotion has had time to soak in she becomes concerned about immediate needs— mostly emotional needs—on the part of both herself and the children that seem threatened. She draws great comfort from having Paul come home from work every evening. It gives her a sense of security to know that he can fix things, or at least call a repairman, when an appliance goes haywire, the roof starts leaking, or the plumbing stops up. She feels safe and fulfilled attending to the "inside chores" when he's keeping the lawn mowed and the cars tuned up.

The children also seem quieter and better behaved when their daddy's around. They need his firm voice in discipline, his gentle strength in play, his wisdom in instruction and counsel. Della sees Paul's promotion as a very real danger to all of these needs.

Paul is not insensitive to these needs. After all, he has emotional and pyschological needs that can be fully met only by his wife and children, too. He needs their love, their closeness, the feeling that they're dependent on him and that he's providing for their needs.

Still, Paul brings more logic than emotion to bear on the situation. He thinks in terms of the long-range well-being of his wife and children. The kids are small now, but the first thing you know they'll be graduating from high school and heading for college. A college education costs a king's ransom these days. Besides, these two may have brothers and sisters before the family stops growing. It takes a lot of money to support a large family and give the kids the educational advantages you want them to have. If he's ever going to rise in income, Paul reasons, he's got to take this job. Nobody has ever advanced very far in his field without progressing through this stage.

It will only last for a few years—three, maybe five at most. It's worth the sacrifice of a few conveniences now in order to assure a more comfortable, financially secure future for the whole family.

But because neither Paul nor Della understand their own

thought processes, and neither knows what built-in inclinations guide the other's reactions, they never talk about these matters.

As a result, Paul makes no special effort to compensate for his absence from the home in order to be sure that the needs of Della and the kids are properly met. When she finds her needs and the children's needs not being fulfilled, Della begins to emphasize these needs to Paul in various ways. She cries a lot. She complains when he's at home about things that happened while he was away, subtly blaming his absence for the problems. To be sure she's getting Paul's attention, she exaggerates the children's troubles. The children, catching on to the game, form the habit of magnifying their problems, making matters still worse.

Still not realizing why things are going as they are, Paul hardens in his determination to stick to his decision. They'll be happy, he tells himself, as soon as they start seeing some of the benefits of his job promotion—more and better clothes, more expensive meals, a bigger house, and maybe even a boat and camper for weekend excursions.

Della never responds in the expected manner. The increase in material wealth doesn't remove her sadness, because her basic needs and those of her children still remain unmet. She becomes even moodier. She begins to hound him to take a cut in pay in order to be at home.

Finally, Paul gives in. He asks for a transfer back to the home office. In so doing, he not only takes a pay cut but also forfeits his hope of ever really getting ahead in his field.

The results are twofold, and both aspects are potentially destructive to the marriage.

First, as part of the deal in his accepting a lower-paying job, Della gets a job outside the home. She has to do so, they reason, if they're to maintain the standard of living they've become accustomed to and have savings enough to send the kids through college.

Neither of them realizes that in depending on the wife for part of the basic financial support of the family they have shifted a portion of Paul's responsibility to Della's shoulders. Some of the problems that creates have already been discussed in another chapter. But one such problem wasn't discussed, and it's the very one that descends upon Paul and Della.

When Paul surrenders some of his responsibility, he assumes some of Della's viewpoint. He ceases to think so much in terms of long-range objectives. He begins, instead, to be concerned about immediate needs.

Della dislikes this arrangement. She's used to leaving the future in Paul's hands. Now, suddenly, nobody seems to be taking care of tomorrow. Della feels more uneasy and insecure now than she did when Paul was traveling. In struggling to get some of her immediate needs met, she has succeeded in assuring that one of her most important needs isn't met—the need to sense that the future is in good hands.

Unable to live with such a situation, Della begins to nag at Paul to stop dwelling so much on immediate needs and start thinking about the long run. But the switch in Paul's orientation is complete. His mind is on immediate needs. Having been pressured into giving up his plans and hopes for the future, he feels resentment when Della tries to get him to concentrate on the years ahead. He construes Della's continual harping on the future as an indication that she's neglecting her responsibilities in the area of immediate needs. Quarreling and unhappiness become the dominant characteristics of their relationship.

Don't miss the twist that has occurred in the roles of Paul and Della and the confusion and discontent it has engendered. Paul has surrendered some of his responsibility and taken on some of Della's viewpoint. Della has assumed part of Paul's responsibility and surrendered some of her viewpoint. The result is that some of the responsibility and some of both viewpoints are not receiving proper attention. Both know something is wrong, but each blames the other for the problems. Each sees only what the other is doing wrong or failing to do without seeing his or her own failures.

All of the problems of Paul and Della could have been avoided if they had understood their respective responsibilities and viewpoints according to God's design for marriage. Della would have had greater appreciation for Paul's concern for the future. He would have realized the significance of her preoccupation with immediate needs. Both could have made the understanding adjustments and compensations the situation demanded.

This is not to say that there wouldn't have been any difficulties. Each might have had to compromise on the basic viewpoint. Each might have had to invoke greater self-discipline to overcome problems raised by the change in family routine.

But the difficulties and the problems could have been overcome—provided the proper spirit had prevailed in the relationship. Actually, the word "Spirit" should begin with a capital "S" because, ultimately, the Spirit that must prevail for a marriage to function according to God's plan is the Holy Spirit.

The necessity for the Holy Spirit to fill and control both partners for a successful marriage is the subject of the next chapter.

THIRTEEN
SPIRITUAL ONENESS

The spirit is the nonphysical part of human nature. It's the center of understanding (1 Cor. 2:11). It's the core of inward reality, as Paul indicates in Romans 2:29, where he speaks of real circumcision being "in the spirit" rather than in the flesh. The human spirit is the seat of man's consciousness. When the man sleeps, his spirit sleeps, the Bible says (Judg. 15:19). It's the center of emotions. Jezebel came to Ahab after he had tried to buy Naboth's vineyard and asked, "Why is thy spirit so sad?" (1 Kgs. 21:5). The spirit is also the source of man's passions. Ezekiel says, " . . . and I went in bitterness, in the heat [anger] of my spirit . . ." (Ezek. 3:14).

What is most important about the human spirit is that it acts upon the will, attempting to force the will to do its bidding in decisions governing attitudes and behavior. " . . . He that ruleth his spirit [is better] than he that taketh a city," God warns in Proverbs 16:32. This fact works against the realization of oneness in the marriage relationship. It does so for two reasons.

First, the human spirit is essentially a self-centered, self-seeking force. It wants to look out for number one. By its very nature, it resists blending in oneness with any other spirit. It's unique, individualistic, and determined to stay that way. When the slightest encroachment is made into its "sphere of influence" by any other spirit, it bristles like a wasp reacting to a stranger approaching its nest.

Secondly, the human spirit defies control by merely human resources. It's almost ludicrous to suggest that the human spirit controls or limits itself, when its primary motivation is self-gratification. A human spirit controls itself only in the sense that it defers gratification when thwarted or, as in the case of Ahab, seeks gratification by another course of action.

It takes little imagination to envision how the human spirit acts to undermine and destroy oneness in marriage. Two essentially selfish, untamable human spirits might have what the world would call a successful marriage if both spirits were convinced that marriage held the best hope for fulfillment of their individual self-interests. That sometimes happens. But with increasing frequency, as the divorce statistics reveal, the results of enclosing two such spirits in the intimacy of a marriage relationship are of the more predictable variety.

CONFLICTING SPIRITS

Clashes between the human spirits of marriage partners occur in an almost infinite variety of ways.

The wife's spirit "naturally" resists the yielding of her will to the will of the husband, as the Bible commands and human tradition supports. When she resists, the husband's spirit reacts with indignation. He may become domineering and try to break his wife's will and force her to yield to his authority. Or he may retreat and let his wife take over, washing his hands of all responsibility for the consequences. If the husband takes the forceful route, he probably will succeed only in causing the wife's spirit to fight back with apathy and bitterness. If he abandons responsibility to her, her spirit may react with contempt toward him. Her spirit does not want to be ruled, and yet it wants to be protected and provided for. When he surrenders responsibility, she feels these needs aren't being met.

The husband's spirit desires admiration and seeks it by giving attention to his career, sports achievements, or perhaps even to other women. The wife's spirit desires to be number one in his life. So intense is that desire that the wife senses it when she is not first place in her husband's life. Her awareness of her husband's infidelity—even when it's only mental—leads to reactions that usually only worsen the problem.

A wife's spirit can antagonize that of a husband if she questions his decisions or shows anxiety over a course of action he has chosen. The spirit of the husband antagonizes that of the wife when he fails to recognize and show appreciation for her attempts to please him.

Because of the essential difference in viewpoints of the wife and husband, discussed earlier, the spirits of the two may clash. Their priorities differ naturally. The spirit of each tends to protect its own priorities. A husband can provoke a resentful reaction in the spirit of his wife by disregarding her opinions or treating them lightly.

An inclination to forgive is not a part of the makeup of the human spirit. A wife or husband can arouse adverse reactions from the spirit of the other by refusing to forgive past injuries or mistakes.

Either party can detect an unforgiving attitude in the other, even when assurance of forgiveness has been given. The human spirit is cunning in turning another person's old mistakes into subtle weapons to bring about desired results. Use of the weapon may take the form of a knowing look or a cutting remark timed to produce the effect that the unforgiving spirit wants. The weapon tends to remain in the arsenal of the spirit even after the unforgiven offense is forgotten. It becomes a way of life. And without fail, except where the patience of God intervenes, it evokes a reaction of resentment in the spirit of the person at whom it is aimed.

Lack of personal discipline on the part of husband or wife supplies fodder for spiritual warfare. A wife who has careless grooming habits, who overeats, or fails to organize and carry out her household duties responsibly invites contempt from her husband. A husband who is a glutton or fails to control his temper or physical appetites creates feelings of hurt and insecurity in his wife's spirit. Usually, she will try to "reform" her husband. That often meets with anger and resentment. The wife's spirit responds with deeper woundedness.

Many spirit clashes occur over the children. The wife's attitudes toward her husband are quickly detected by the children. If her spirit is fearful or distrusting, the children learn to be wary of their father. This impedes his communications with them. Often, this subtle (and usually unconscious) teaching of the children is accompanied by a developing sense of alliance between the mother and children against the father. Though he may not recognize the nature of the problem, the father detects in his spirit that he is a second-class citizen in his own household. His spirit naturally stirs with resentment, leading to continuous quarrels and clashes involving both the wife and the children.

Inconsistent disciplining of the children gives rise to spirit clashes, also. Many times, the husband shoulders the blame for this fault. When he comes home in an ugly mood, he flies off the handle over the slightest annoyance created by the children. When he's in a jolly mood, he tends to let them get by with almost anything short of mayhem. This arouses frustration and anger in the spirit of the wife.

Since she's the one who attends to the children most of the time the wife usually has laid down some rules of behavior which she tries to enforce. A husband who attempts to undermine these rules by being too lenient engenders anger in the spirit of his wife. He may also stir suspicion, because she may think he is trying to win the children's favor at her expense.

The problem also works in reverse, of course. If the wife tends to be lenient in disciplining the children, the husband may become suspicious, especially if she interferes when he starts to punish a child for disobedience.

Ingratitude causes many spirit clashes. The self-nature, because it wants everything for itself, tends to take everything it receives as something it richly deserves. In fact, it tends to feel that even the best it receives isn't quite enough. So the human spirit rarely feels or displays genuine gratitude. Or it does so hypocritically, because it has learned that showing gratitude leads to more favors. The ungrateful attitude leaves the other partner feeling that every favor he or she bestows is "expected," that nothing can ever produce a pleasantly surprised reaction. This leads to emotional scars and eventually to loss of desire to please.

Spirit clashes that spill over into the public domain compound the damages caused by the problem. Feeling unable to win the spirit battle in the arena of the home, the wife or husband's spirit seeks unwitting allies among friends or even strangers. This usually takes the form of jokes or cutting remarks aimed at the other partner in the presence of other people. Wounds inflicted by such attacks only arouse vengeful motives in the spirit of the afflicted party. Retaliation leads to counterattack, and the destructive cycle rages on.

The root of the problem of clashing spirits in marriage is defined in numerous passages of Scripture. Proverbs outlines it most sharply.

"All the ways of a man are clean in his own eyes; but the Lord weigheth the spirits [motives]," says Proverbs 16:2.

Proverbs 21:2 is almost an exact repetition: "Every way of a man is right in his own eyes: but the Lord pondereth the hearts."

The prophet Jeremiah puts his finger on the kernel of the problem in the often quoted verse: "The heart [of the natural man] is deceitful above all things, and desperately wicked: who can know it?" (Jer. 17:9).

The problem, clearly, is that the human spirit or human heart thinks it knows what's best for it but actually does not. It's deceived. Its priorities are warped. Its sense of values is hopelessly distorted.

In his volumes, *The Spiritual Man,* the Chinese evangelist Watchman Nee gives a detailed anatomy of the problem. To summarize Nee's insight, he says that God created the spirit to be the place of his throne in the human makeup. The soul, seat of the mind, emotion, and will, was to be enlightened and controlled continuously by God's action through the spirit. When man disobeyed God and fell into sin, however, the soul usurped the controlling responsibilities God had reserved for himself. The result is that man's only true motivation is to serve himself. In so doing, he actually doesn't understand the devices his own heart is using to drive and direct him.

Do you wonder why so few really happy marriages are found among non-Christians? How could two essentially self-serving creatures achieve the oneness that produces an enduring, fulfilling marriage?

THE WAY TO ONENESS

The only solution to the human dilemma of the clashing spirits is the answer that God offers through Christ.

Jeremiah refers to that answer right after asking his dismal question, "Who can know it [the human heart]?" The next verse says:

"I the Lord search the heart."

Only God knows the heart. Only God can control the heart.

After he had sinned grievously, King David prayed: "Create in me a clean heart, O God; and renew a right spirit within me" (Psa. 51:10).

If spirit clashes are destroying your marriage, you can start solving the problem this instant by praying that same prayer. It's a prayer of repentance. You recognize that you've usurped God's place in your life—that you've been in the driver's seat and that you're speeding toward disaster. Commit your life to Jesus Christ, acknowledge him as Savior and Lord of your life and resolve to follow and obey him. Ask him to create a clean heart in you. Ask him to create a right spirit in you, a spirit severed from the puppet strings of a selfish soul and filled and guided by the Spirit of God.

Your husband or wife may or may not make this commitment with you. It would be tremendous if you could make it together. Then both would be ruled by one Spirit—the Holy Spirit. But if your mate refuses to go along with you, step out in faith on your own and trust God to do his part.

First, God will heal your own life and make you whole. If you'll study his Word, if you'll prayerfully obey his directions, he will give you what it takes to live a Holy Spirit-controlled life in your home.

When you are living a Spirit-controlled life, God will perform his work on your mate. Your Godly, love-filled life can be used of the Lord to bring about changes in the heart of your partner. The going may get rough, because your mate may come under conviction of the Holy Spirit. The selfish human spirit sometimes fights bitterly when it senses its domain being invaded by another Authority. It resists the encroachment on its autonomy. In some instances, the marriage relationship actually deteriorates. If that happens, the only consolation you have is that there was no hope for it with two selfish spirits warring against each other.

In most cases, I believe I can say, however, that the outcome is beautiful. In time, the second partner bows down to the Lordship of Christ. Then, with both spirits controlled by the same Spirit, the warfare ends and the building of spiritual oneness at last can begin. It's a thrill to see two people discover the joy of oneness in Christ after years of spiritual strife.

Unfortunately, it's not only lost couples who waste years of marriage in clashes of the spirit. Many born-again Christians never grow spiritually. They receive Christ as Savior and Lord but, for one reason or another, they fail to give him full control of their lives.

In the human spirit, there's no such thing as a vacuum. If the Holy Spirit isn't in control, then the Devil is in control through the selfish human spirit. The Devil also controls believers when they do not yield to the Holy Spirit.

Believers, in fact, may be even more miserable than unbelievers when they reject the control of the Holy Spirit. The reason is simple. They're God's children. God doesn't leave his children alone when they're in a non-repentant state. He works on them to bring them to repentance. Sometimes he uses stern measures, actions that produce unpleasantness and discontent.

Even though you're a Christian, your solution to the problem of clashing spirits is essentially the same as that of the lost person. You must repent of your self-centered ways, turn to God for forgiveness, and let him fill your heart with his love and wisdom. "Christ in you, the [only] hope of glory" (Col. 1:27).

FOURTEEN
PHYSICAL ONENESS

" . . . Now the body is not for fornication, but for the Lord; and the Lord for the body" (1 Cor. 6:13).

I know this verse refers to unlawful sex; it means that your body is not made for sexual indulgence. Your body was made to glorify God.

While the verse applies directly to sex outside marriage, I'm convinced that it has application to sex in marriage, as well. Sex is so overemphasized and overglorified in modern society that its importance, even within the marriage relationship, has become hideously distorted. Putting too much store in sex, and depending on sexual ecstasy more than on God to cement togetherness, has led to the downfall of many marriages.

As we've already said, sex is the means provided by God for a man and woman to develop physical oneness. It's a beautiful gift that makes interpersonal unity possible. It's also the means God has provided for physical perpetuation of the race.

SEX IS NOT MARRIAGE

Sex is a wonderful, intimate way to express love. Love has its thrilling emotional and psychological side-effects, and these are sometimes mistaken for "the real thing." But the real thing is commitment to meeting the needs of another. Since sex is an important means of expressing love in marriage, then, sex properly engaged in is a precious means of meeting needs.

However, while sex practiced according to God's plan is an expression of love, it is not love itself.

Is it any wonder that many marriages are falling apart in these times? Though sex is only part of the love and marriage relationship, millions of couples treat it as if it were everything. Because of the distorted emphasis our society places on it, sex has become a god, even in marriage. Couples trust it to patch up their differences, fulfill their inward desires and hold them together in the face of all the forces pulling them apart.

STRATEGIES OF CONFUSION

The world uses different strategies at different times in an attempt to deify sex. For many generations, the romantic aspects of love were exalted and glorified to create confusion about the true meaning of love.

Romantic love produced some of the richest literature in the languages of men. It inspired enrapturing lyrics and beautiful melodies. And let me quickly add that I do not believe there is anything wrong or sinful about the romantic aspect of love, *as such*. After all, Songs of Solomon and other Scripture passages acknowledge that romance plays a significant part in the husband-wife relationship. God uses such passages to illustrate the devotion and intimacy of the relationship he desires to have with those who love him.

However, the Devil has twisted the romantic aspect of love out of context. With the beautiful lyrics and rhapsodic melodies, he has deceived millions into believing that romance and the intense feelings that go with it are all there is to love. He has given us the phrase "in love" to describe the giddy emotionalism of romantic love. A strong desire for sexual intimacy, though cloaked with sweet words and music, usually is very much a part of being "in love."

Sociological studies sometimes leave me cold—in fact, they sometimes leave me furious. But one that I read recently can be helpful to us, I think, in understanding the harm that can be done by the confusion between the romantic aspect of love and love itself. The study revealed that the powerful emotions identified as the signs of being "in love" last no longer than six to thirty months.

Do you see the significance of that finding? If a husband believes that being "in love" is all there is to love, when the "in love" feelings wear thin in the intimacy of marriage, he is going to believe he no longer loves his wife. The same fate can befall a wife who doesn't understand the difference between love's romantic aura and love itself.

Thus, the all too common phenomenon of husbands and wives telling their mates—out of the clear blue—"I don't love you any more."

Another strategy Satan has used is to deceive people into believing that love is merely the gratification of physical appetites through sexual relations. This strategy has become more prominent in recent years. As young people have become disillusioned with the romantic love that has failed so many of their parents, they have fallen for the Devil's line that love is nothing more than physical sex. Most of them have so little faith in purely sensual love, though, that they refuse to make longterm commitments to one partner. Gratifying physical appetites too often requires exchanging familiar partners for strange ones who, it is hoped, will provide new and more exhilarating thrills. Even when couples with this mistaken concept of love do marry, the relationship is doomed to disillusionment and dissolution. Love is not simply gratification of sensual desires.

SEXUAL RESPONSIBILITIES

Into every relationship he has designed, God has built responsibilities for those who participate. Marriage is no exception. The first responsibility, always, is to God himself. God reserves the right to be God in everything. He—not sex— is God in the marriage relationship. He must be the object of worship to both partners in the marriage, not the thrill or the temporary physical gratification sex produces. Sex in marriage, like any other activity, is to be exercised under God's control. God cannot bless marriages in which sex is the reigning deity. Making sex a god is idolatry. God will not excuse it.

The second responsibility is to the family of God and to the lost.

The Apostle Paul says, in 1 Corinthians 7:2, that, to avoid fornication, every man should have his own wife and every

woman her own husband. Fornication, sex practiced in a
manner not ordained of God, is a degenerative and destructive
lifestyle. It dishonors God. When committed by God's children,
it brings a terrible judgment of unhappiness and personal
tragedy. It dismantles families and causes bitter disharmony
among believers. The witness of Christians who are involved
in fornication or who condone it produces a negative impact.
Instead of drawing sinners to Christ, it drives them away. It
denies to the lost opportunities to see and hear the Lord and
come to repentance.

Because of its destructive impact, fornication also
undermines the moral foundations of society as a whole. Thus,
Paul uttered a very serious bit of instruction to the early
believers when he advised them to marry and be faithful to
their own husbands and wives.

The third responsibility in marriage is that which marriage
partners are to exercise toward each other. The passage just
quoted goes on to say:

"Let the husband render unto the wife due benevolence [that
which she rightly deserves]: and likewise also the wife unto the
husband.

"The wife hath not power of [is not master over] her own
body, but the husband: and likewise also the husband hath not
power of [is not master over] his own body, but the wife.

"Defraud [deprive] ye not one the other, except it be with
consent for a time, that ye may give yourselves to fasting and
prayer; and come together again, that Satan tempt you not for
your incontinency" (1 Cor. 7:3-5).

In marriage, God's style, two people are to literally give
themselves to each other. The giving is to be so complete that
they don't even consider themselves to be masters over their
own bodies. It's a "his" and "hers" arrangement. His body
belongs to her. Her body belongs to him. She is not to
withhold her body from him, and he is not to withhold his
body from her, without mutual consent. If this principle is
violated, Paul warns that the marriage partners will be
exposing themselves to temptation by Satan.

Such total surrender requires love—real love, total
commitment to meeting each other's needs. Proverbs 5:18-19
paints a beautiful picture of how this applies in the meeting of
physical needs:

" . . . Rejoice with the wife of thy youth. Let her be as the loving hind and pleasant roe; let her breasts satisfy thee at all times; and be thou ravished always with her love."

The message is addressed to the husband, but clearly it encompasses both partners. A husband can't "rejoice with" his wife unless she also rejoices. The instruction to "let her be as the loving hind and pleasant roe" assumes that she is willing to fulfill that role as a responding, participating partner in love. "Let her breasts satisfy thee . . .and be thou ravished [exhilarated] always with her love" assumes that she will be attempting, in full devotion, to be a pleasing mate to her husband.

The passage in Corinthians also makes plain the fact that God created both husband and wife with physical and psychological needs which their marriage partners have a responsibility to meet.

You will notice that Paul did not merely say to wives, "Defraud not your husbands," as though only husbands had a need for physical sex. Nor did he merely say, "Husbands, defraud not your wives." He said, "Defraud ye not one the other." Each has physical needs, and each has a responsibility to the other to meet those needs.

Needless to say, this rules out the little games some people play in marriage, in which one partner uses sex as a weapon to manipulate the other. Sex has been given as a means to meet needs, not as a device for one to use in getting his or her own way.

Concerning this responsibility, let me interject one word of warning. As surely as sex should never be used as a weapon, neither should it be looked upon as a duty.

When having sex with your marriage partner seems a duty, rather than a delightful expression of love, it's time for you to read some of the earlier chapters of this book and try to discover what the problem is. The descriptions of husband-wife love found in the Scriptures never depict it as drudgery. God plainly intended it to be a joyful, exhilarating experience. If it is not, something is wrong.

Expressing love in sex also requires each partner to respect the desires and preferences of the other and to be sensitive to the other's moods and physical condition.

At times, either the husband or the wife will have a greater need for some other expression of love than for a sexual expression of love. When a husband comes home after a dispute on the job, a great disappointment, or a very tiring day, he may not be emotionally or physically capable of expressing love sexually. He may have a greater need for a comforting, reassuring expression of love from his wife. Wives who have had difficulties with the children, a hard day of washing clothes and cleaning house may need an expression of appreciation and encouragement more than an expression of sexual love.

Marriage partners who are sensitive to their mates' real needs and their various moods will be rewarded for their patience and understanding. By not trying to force their partners into physical love when they don't desire it, they prove to them that their love is genuine, that they don't want their mates merely for sex. Sexual love then becomes more meaningful and fulfilling, because it becomes a true expression of oneness.

Achieving physical oneness requires an adjustment of each partner to the other. The degree of aggressiveness and passiveness, roughness and tenderness that is mutually pleasing must be found through experimentation. Provided each partner keeps in mind that the object of sexual expression is to please and fulfill the needs of the other partner, this physical oneness can be accomplished without disagreeble consequences.

Couples should continue their search for pleasing expressions of love throughout their lives together. There is no reason for sexual expression to fall victim to boredom.

At this point, though, I must sound another word of warning. As I've said repeatedly, sex is not love. Sexual gratification can be overemphasized even within the marriage bond. It should never be treated as an end in itself, but only as a means to an end—that of expressing love.

Men and women are exposed to many thoughts and ideas about sexual conduct today—through magazines and other media, through contact with other persons on their jobs and in their social lives and even in the "how-to" sex manuals sold at newsstands. Some of these thoughts and ideas may prompt a husband or wife (my counseling experiences indicate that it is usually the husband) to suggest sexual behavior that their mate finds offensive.

A simple rule of love applies in such cases. The rule of love is stated in 1 Corinthians 13:5: Love "seeketh not her own." That is, love does not seek to gratify its own desires at the expense of another. A husband who loves his wife will never try to force her into behavior that she considers objectionable. That simply isn't the way to express love.

Husbands, or wives, who continually desire strange, new sexual thrills probably should review earlier discussions of impurity and guilty conscience. Often, insatiable sexual desire points to past behavior and present character traits that prevent development of oneness in marriage. That, of course, spells deep trouble for the marriage. Disaster can be forestalled only if the basic problem is solved through repentance, personal commitment to Christ and the cleansing of the Holy Spirit.

CONTINUING COURTSHIP

Finally, husbands and wives should remember their courtship—and continue it throughout their marriage.

Sexual oneness certainly is important to marital happiness. It provides confidence and fulfillment for the husband. It strengthens a wife's sense of security and worthiness. But a wife needs the tenderness and thoughtfulness she received during courtship all through her married life to keep her assured that her husband finds her total personality desirable, not merely her physical body. And the husband needs continually to be shown the respect and consideration he received from the woman he courted, who always presented herself to him clean, well groomed and attractive.

Ironically, marriage partners who consistently prove that sexual gratification is not their only goal in marriage are far more likely to find sexual gratification than those who do have sex as their only goal.

God honors those who trust him and do things his way.

Those who reject him and refuse to follow him are only cheating themselves.

THIRTY-FIVE years ago, a boy was born in the charity ward of a Texas hospital. Three weeks later his divorced and impoverished mother placed an ad in a local newspaper offering him to someone who would give him love and a home. The odds are about a thousand to one against a boy like that making it in life, but the child who grew up to become evangelist James Robison not only has changed his personal destiny, but is helping millions of all ages, from all walks of life, to trade in their own troubled existences for lives of inner peace through Jesus Christ.

Responding to the newspaper ad, Rev. and Mrs. H. D. Hale of Pasadena, Texas, took James into their home where he lived for the first five years of his life. He then spent ten years in Austin with his mother during difficult years upset by a stepfather who had become an alcoholic.

With his mother's permission, James returned to live with the Hales and finish high school where he played for two years on the school's varsity football team. On an earlier visit to their home he had committed his life to Jesus Christ at Memorial Baptist Church in Pasadena. It was a sincere though unspectacular commitment. Three years later, when James was eighteen, Jesus Christ showed him that he had specific plans for his life. Although James had been planning to study law at the University of Texas, he accepted God's call to become an evangelist and he enrolled at East Texas Baptist College in Marshall. During his first year in college he began preaching evangelistic meetings and by age nineteen had received over 1,000 invitations to conduct revival meetings in twenty-seven states.

Attendance records were broken during citywide crusades in football stadiums and auditoriums across America as God moved mightily. James Robison has now spoken to more than nine million people face-to-face in over 450 crusades throughout the United States. Millions more see him weekly on the nationally syndicated telecast "Man with a Message." More than 300,000 people have responded publicly to his challenge to invite Jesus Christ into their lives.

James Robison has an immediate rapport with young people, having spoken to over 200,000 of them in high school assemblies each year. His preaching style is uncompromising and exuberant, yet he is an unassuming family man anxious to spend time with his wife, Betty, and their three children. He enjoys hunting and fishing for relaxation.

In recent times, Robison has unfolded his vision to bring the Word of God to America through prime-time television broadcasts coast-to-coast. He is emphatic that he is not trying to replace the church, but desires to help revive and build it through the outreach of these televised crusades. As he explains, "God has given me to understand that the times are desperate—that I must warn the people, that I must not—and will not—compromise his Word!"